Body Sense

Body Sense

EXERCISE FOR RELAXATION

Margit Haxthausen and Rhea Leman

FOREWORD BY ALEXANDER LOWEN M.D.

PHOTOGRAPHS BY CLAUS KNUDTSKOV

Pantheon Books   New York

LIBRARY OF CONGRESS CATALOGING-IN-PUBLICATION DATA
Haxthausen, Margit, 1949–
Body sense.
Translation of: Krop.
Bibliography: p.
1. Movement education. 2. Dancing. 3. Exercise.
I. Leman, Rhea, 1954–   . II. Title.
GV452.H3913   1987   613.7   86-25325
ISBN 0-394-74917-0

CONTENTS

Foreword	7
Preface	8
Afspaending	10
Do You Notice How You're Feeling?	12
Tensing/Relaxing	14
Breathing	16
The Body's Axes	17
Basic Supine Position	18
Supine Stretching	19
Legs Above Your Stomach	20
Basic Sitting Position	21
Arching Movements on a Chair	21
Rounding Movements on a Chair	22
Arm Movements	22
Basic Standing Position	23
Standing Pendulum	23
Accordion	24
Roll Down from Standing Up	24
Standing Stretches	25
Pillows in Rest Positions	26
How Do You Use the Movements?	27
Movements 1	29
Basic Lying-Down Movements	30
Stretch Up to Your Heels	30
Moving Your Pelvis with Your Stomach	31

Moving Your Pelvis with Your Buttocks	31
Moving Your Pelvis with the Pelvic Floor and Stomach	31
Moving Your Pelvis Starting from Your Legs	32
Basic Sitting Movements	33
Sitting Flower	34
Half-Flower	34
Half-Sitting Pendulum	35
The Cat	36
The Role of the Helper	37
Variation of the Cat	37
Stretch Forward and Breathe	37
Basic Standing Movements	39
Rotate from Your Ankle Joint	39
The Carousel	39
Dynamic Arm-Stretching to the Sides	40
Javanese Variation	41
Dynamic Forward Arm-Stretching	41
The Ski Movement	43
Legs on a Big Pillow	43
Movements 2	45
Lying Movements	46
Lying Flower	46
Hip Swing	47
Chaplin	47
The Worm	48
Working with a Partner	48
Prone Position	49
Sea Lion	50

Sea Lion with Hands on Floor	50
The Cat Stretch	51
Sitting Movements (Floor)	53
Seated Hamstring Stretches	53
Hanging Forward	53
The Cradle	53
Squatting	54
Standing Movements	56
Shift Weight and Balance	56
Stretch Forward and Pull Back	57
Roll Down from a Standing Position	58
Standing Stretch	59
Sitting Movements (Chair)	60
Feel the Weight in Each Other's Legs	60
Feel the Weight in Each Other's Arms	61
Chair Arch	61
The Shoulder Elevator	61
Lowering Your Shoulders	61
Neck and Head Rotation	62
Hanging Forward	62
Getting Up	64
Foot Movements	65
The Foot's Mobility	65
Rotation of Toes	65
Push with Your Toes	65
Walking	66
The Senses of Your Feet	66
The Foot's Mobility in Walking	66
Balloon Walking	66

Modern Dance	69	Forward with Stretched Legs	94	From Side to Side	119
		Second Position	96	Extension and Release	120
Warm-Up 1	71	Variations in Second Position	96	Torso and Leg Swings	120
Movement Combinations: Lying		First Variation in Second			
Down	72	Position	96	*Standing Movement Combinations:*	
Find the Floor	72	Second Variation in Second		*A Wrap-Up*	122
Divide Your Body	73	Position	97		
Turn-Out	73	Third Variation in Second		**Warm-Up 4**	123
Pointing the Foot	74	Position	97	*Movement Combinations: Rhythmic*	124
Flexing the Foot	74	Fourth Variation in Second		First Combination	125
Combining Movements	75	Position	98	Second Combination	126
Grow Through Your Legs	75	Variations on the Variations	99	Third Combination	127
The "Center"—Your Body's		Stretch in Second Position	100	Fourth Combination	128
Energy Point	77	Stand Up	100	Fifth Combination	129
Opening Out	78			Sixth Combination	130
Connecting Parallel and Turned-		*Sitting Movement Combinations:*			
Out Positions Through Space	78	*A Wrap-Up*	102	*A Few Final Words*	134
Borrowing from the Past	79				
Moving Your Legs and Feet		**Warm-Up 3**	103	*Further Reading*	135
Through Space	79	*Movement Combinations: Standing*	104		
Fetal Position	81	The Standing Positions	104		
Lifting Your Torso	82	First Position Parallel	104		
		First Position Turn-Out	105		
Lying-Down Combinations:		Second Position Parallel	105		
A Wrap-Up	83	Second Position Turn-Out	105		
1. Breathing	83	Combine the Positions	105		
2. Rhythm	83	Plié	105		
3. Focus	84	Relevé	108		
		Combine the Movements	108		
Warm-Up 2	85	Your Leg Through Space	109		
Movement Combinations: Sitting	86	Leg Swing	111		
Soles of the Feet Together	86	Swing with Stretched Legs	112		
Your Arms	87	Swing Forward and Backward			
The Anchor	88	with Your Legs	114		
Swinging	90	Your Head as a Weight	115		
Sideways Stretch	92	Standing Swing	116		
Swing from Side to Side	93	Swing with Relevé	118		

FOREWORD

The current interest in the body follows two paths: one leads toward the goal of making the body fit to perform, the other toward a body that is alive and sensitive. If the emphasis is upon fitness to perform, whether in sports or another activity, then the body is seen as a machine with the ideal being 100 percent efficiency. When the focus is upon aliveness and sensitivity, the body is seen as the incarnation of the spirit. The ideal is a body that is capable of fully expressing a person's feelings and emotions and of fully responding to the feelings of others. Such a body is characterized by its natural beauty and grace, by a softness of manner and an ease of movement. The efficient body is characterized by physical strength, endurance, and effectiveness of movement; its keynote is action, whereas feeling inspires the sensitive body.

However, the two goals—fitness to perform and sensitivity to feeling—are not mutually exclusive, unless they are pushed to extremes. A healthy body can be both strong and sensitive, effective in its movements and yet moving with ease, in control and yet spontaneously alive. In fact, one would have to say that unless both aspects are present, one cannot consider the body to be healthy. This is actually the natural state of all animal organisms, for if they were neither effective in their movements nor sensitive to their environment, they would not survive in the wild. Human beings are different. We don't live in the wild, in the true state of nature, but in an environment that is a creation of culture. Our strength is greatly magnified through the power of the machine, and our control over nature has grown to an almost unimaginable degree. Living in this environment, our bodies have lost many of the qualities that mark the wild animal: they are rigid, tight, and stiff in their movements. Simply stated, our bodies are not in good shape or good health.

We realize, then, that we need to do some physical exercises to restore the health of our bodies, to regain a good shape. But which exercises we do will depend upon our view of the body. If we see it as an instrument of the will, as a mechanism for action, we will choose exercises that develop our muscles in the direction of strength and control. Health, in this view, is equated with a firm, hard body and a tough, aggressive psychological attitude. Softness is a sign of weakness, even sickness. In a tight, hard body, feelings are denied and suppressed. In the opposite view, the body is seen as the source of feelings, as a vehicle for the expression of feelings, and health is equated with liveliness and sensitivity. The exercises chosen will be those that require the person to feel what is happening in the body as it moves. Such exercises cannot be done mechanically, so they cannot be done with an exercise machine. If done properly, they produce a body that has its strength in its lively softness, not in rigidity, that has poise and self-possession rather than control. I do not regard the overdeveloped, muscular body as healthy. Bodily rigidity is a sign of death, not life. In death one becomes totally rigid. To the degree that we can avoid becoming rigid, we stay younger, healthier, and more open to pleasure.

Body Sense belongs to this second view of the body. The exercises it offers are soft and designed to further one's awareness of the body and its possible movements. They employ many stretches, to expand the body and free it from tension. Forcing is avoided, as this tends to distort the body. Breathing is emphasized, for the body becomes rigid when the breath is held. Above all, the reader is urged to pay attention to the feeling in the body—to feel the body as it goes through the movements of the various exercises. These exercises can lead to a body that is healthier and more capable of performing well in all activities—especially those involving the expression of feeling, as in drama and in modern dance.

Alexander Lowen, M.D.

PREFACE TO THE AMERICAN EDITION

A woman executive has been sitting in the same chair in the same position, week after week. Her back hurts. She goes to a physical therapist for a massage, but her pain returns after each treatment.

A man in the same office works out every day to achieve the flat belly he sees advertised around him. But no matter how much sweat he works up, he fails to arrive at the physique he wants.

What are they doing wrong? Despite their best intentions, they're not listening to their bodies. If they would, they'd know that massage is only a temporary solution to the tensions that plague us, and that vigorous exercise is not the only way to tone our muscles. Body sense—an awareness of the ways in which we use and misuse our body—is as vital to our well-being as any fitness regimen. When we listen to our bodies, we know instinctively how best to move, when to push ourselves, and when to stop. Yet body sense isn't easily achieved at a gym, or during a workout, or even at the hands of a skilled physical therapist. That's why we're so pleased to have before us the American edition of this book—because it allows us to bring the Danish method of body awareness called *afspaending* to American readers.

Afspaending is the most effective way we know to develop coordination and elasticity. Both of us use it in our work—Margit as a relaxation therapist, and Rhea as a dancer. On a practical level it enables people to use the muscles and joints gracefully and with as little wear-and-tear as possible. On another level, it attunes them to the many ways in which the emotions affect their experience of their bodies. Much of the tension we feel in our backs, necks, and shoulders may be attributed to the fact that we are creatures of habit who lie, sit, and stand in the same positions day after day. But some of the stiffness we feel can be traced back to feelings we are trying to ignore. When we become aware of the ways in which these feelings virtually inhabit our bodies, much of this tension melts away.

As you'll see when you practice them, the movements that make up afspaending can help straighten a rounded back or flatten bulging abdominal muscles. They can also help lower shoulders that have hiked up, relax a tense neck, and tuck in a protruding bottom. How? By promoting good alignment. Simply learning to use the hip joints properly can change the look of the entire body. The goal of afspaending, though, is not to make you look twenty years younger than you are, but to help you relax and to give you a feeling of ease in movement. It is inevitable that you will end up appreciating your body more.

The first section of the book, written by Margit, explains afspaending in words and pictures. The second, written by Rhea, shows you how to combine what you've learned with movements from modern dance. Afspaending will be your foundation and starting point for the fast, rhythmic movements of dance. In the afspaending movements, you will sense where and how you can use your body without unnecessary tension and when you should stop in order not to tense up against the movements. Keep these experiences in mind when you begin working with dance, and use those afspaending movements that help you get in touch with the muscles you find most difficult to use in the different dance movements illustrated.

The marriage of afspaending with modern dance is a natural one, because both require an understanding not only of the body's abilities, but also of its limits. It makes no sense to push your body beyond what you can comfortably accomplish. But with patient effort, and a willingness to work with your joints and muscles rather than against them, you can develop an entirely different relationship to your body that will stand you in good stead as you pursue other forms of exercise, as you sit at work, and as you move through your day.

Margit Haxthausen
Rhea Leman
Copenhagen

P REFACE

We met each other by chance a few years ago and immediately became very interested in each other's way of working with the body. After deciding to try to work together, we found considerable similarities and parallels in our training, despite our very different methods of teaching.

We both work with movement based on the composition and construction of the joints and muscles and how these influence each other. For both of us, part of the goal of our teaching is to expand and vary the ways our students experience their bodies, at the same time improving their overall functioning. We attempt to reach this goal through movements that enable the students to feel how the various groups of muscles function and how they are interrelated.

The movements of modern dance, its elasticity and constant exchange between tension, stretching, and relaxing, are related to the types of movement that are used in afspaending.

Those who have become inspired through afspaending to continue working with their bodies this way will be able to experience the dance section in a more outwardly aesthetic and visual way. Working with dance can also provide vital muscular strength, which isn't necessarily achieved through afspaending. This strength may subsequently influence the afspaending

movements and make some of them easier, as it requires less effort to coordinate movements when the various groups of muscles are of equal strength.

Through the very slow, analytical movements of afspaending, students of modern dance are able to sense how they use their bodies and what their limits are. Working individually with these movements, they can develop a greater and more detailed understanding of the ways the various groups of muscles function and feel and in what way they influence each other, all without having to concentrate on the aesthetic element of modern dance.

Afspaending will be your foundation and starting point for the fast rhythmic movements of modern dance in the second half of the book. In the afspaending movements, you will sense where and how you can use your body without unnecessary tension, and you will sense when you should stop in order not to tense up against movements. Keeping the experience of the afspaending movements in mind when you begin working with dance will help you get in touch with the muscles you find difficult to use in the various dance movements.

We will point out when the afspaending movements can be used in connection with certain dance movements, yet it will always be up to each individual to decide what seems appro-

priate and at what point it should be used. You should always proceed with the movements based on what you feel, and use them in a way that is right for you.

Because you are working from a book, your knowledge of these movements must travel via your intellect to your body, which may seem paradoxical. In addition to this, we take certain experiences for granted, otherwise the descriptions would be too long and confusing. Yet we always encourage you to use what you experience with your own body as a guide, both in terms of how you should proceed, and in sensing what your limits are.

If you use and respect what you feel, your experiences can eventually become integrated within yourself, and these new ways of moving will become a natural part of your daily life.

—M.H. and R.L.

A F S P A E N D I N G

Afspaending—a Danish word for "un-buckling," "relaxing," pronounced ow(f)*spain*(d)ing—was started in 1940 by three Danish women with backgrounds in drama and movement.

It took years before afspaending was recognized as a preventive and therapeutic form of treatment, yet within the past 10 years both the interest in and practice of afspaending have grown tremendously. Today, Danish doctors, psychiatrists, and psychologists often suggest afspaending to their patients as part of the treatment for somatic as well as psychological illnesses. The underlying premise of afspaending is that the body and the psyche form an indivisible whole, so that the functioning of the body influences the psyche, and vice versa.

This attitude leads to a greater respect for the way each person uses his or her body, as well as the conviction that lasting, fruitful results can be achieved through positive experiences. That is why there is never any sort of force or pressure used in afspaending.

Afspaending movements are slow, with attention paid to the feelings in the body. All feelings are equally important, including what feels like resistance.

The goal is not to achieve a beautiful figure. You will achieve a greater understanding of how you use your body, and an awareness of a changing balance of tension in it. You will be able to get rid of aches and pains and feel more life in your body.

Because afspaending is oriented toward the individual, it can be used successfully by people of both sexes and all ages.

Activities involving afspaending can be divided into three groups: fundamental positions, treatment, and movement. This book describes and deals with the fundamental positions and movements, which everyone can work with on their own.

You are going to work with your body in a way that involves your entire self, and that also will involve much more of your time and attention than you'll spend reading this book.

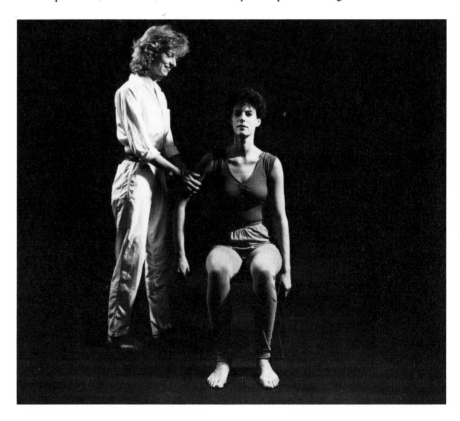

You are going to listen to your body and pay attention to the signals it sends you about your feelings and actions. The starting point for such a process always depends on the individual, but not matter where you are today, the way you experience your body can be improved and expanded.

To be able to experience your own body doesn't necessarily mean that you can do lots of new things with it. The way you experience your body depends upon your ability to sense not only what you can do but also what you cannot do, and also to sense when you meet resistance in experiencing your feelings and reactions.

The attempt to expand the limits of your abilities is the first step in changing yourself. You must learn to sense your limits and respect them. That's why it's important not to push yourself in the movements. Pushing yourself may increase your resistance and make you tense up even more. Change of any kind is more difficult in these circumstances.

If you work slowly and attentively with the movements, you will be able to sense how to relax your muscles and let the movements stretch them. You will also see how you resist movement, thus preventing the muscles from stretching. You will be able to sense which groups of muscles are elastic enough that you can use them actively without tightening them unnecessarily, and which muscles and joints are stretched, to the point where they slow down or block your execution of a movement.

By using what you have and working with what you experience, you take part in an ongoing process that will eventually improve your body's overall functioning. The movements of af-spaending are designed with this in mind.

D O Y O U N O T I C E
H O W Y O U ' R E F E E L I N G ?

Your muscles and tendons have sensory cells that tell you when they're being stretched or put under pressure. As a result, you're aware of the relative position of the parts of your body, the strain placed on them, and the extent to which you've tensed your muscles. This is why you don't have to look under the table to see where you've placed your legs, and why you can sense whether the position feels comfortable or is tiring.

If the muscles' sensory cells detect any strain that could damage the muscle or joint, the muscles react by tensing up. It is this reflex that, for example, prevents you from dislocating your shoulder if you are suddenly pulled by the arm.

Your state of mind affects the level of your muscular reactions. Nervousness, anxiety, anger, or pain will often cause you to react with increased tension in the muscles, so you automatically tense up against even quite small amounts of stretching. On the other hand, the amount of tension, and consequently your muscles' resistance, can be decreased if you feel good about what you're doing.

Everyone is able to feel where and how the parts of their bodies are in relation to each other so that they can coordinate their movements—cooperation between muscles is necessary, with some muscles working and others relaxing so they don't resist the movement.

Such coordination is not instinctive, but is developed through countless repetitions of movements. This is one of the reasons why you can't count on being able to do the afspaending and modern dance movements simply by studying the pictures. Only after going through the movements many times and acquiring an inner feeling about them will you be able to execute them with ease.

When you change the way you use your body, your muscles change the signals they send you, too. It may feel strange, but stay with it.

Try it: Stand up!

Like most people, your toes are probably pointing more or less outward.

Now stand with your feet parallel, your toes pointing straight ahead. Does it feel strange—as if you've become incredibly knock-kneed, or as if your behind sticks out much too much?

It is your senses that are telling you something is different, and the unfamiliar always feels strange.

Feeling how you relate to your body and how you use it doesn't just come from the movements alone. Look upon the movements as tools that can get you started and as an inspiration to continue improving your relationship to your own body.

In your daily life, occasionally give yourself time to direct your attention inward to feel what your body is telling you. This isn't to say that you must shut out your surroundings. Just the opposite. Being aware of yourself and relating to what you feel can often help you be even more aware of other people and their situations.

Try to concentrate on yourself during various times of the day.

When you wake up in the morning: How are you lying? Do you feel comfortable, or could you loosen up some of your muscles?

Without using a lot of energy, try to stretch long and steadily on one side at a time. How are you lying now?

How does it feel when you walk on the street? Can you feel the mobility of your feet, that you have heels and toes?

Try to start your steps heel down first. Use your feet to push you forward and let your arms swing with the movement.

When you sit: How are you resting on your behind? How do your thighs feel against the chair and your feet against the floor?

Go through your entire body: your back, neck and head, shoulders, arms and hands. Are you sitting well? Can you sit better by moving a little? Do you feel that you need to fidget?

Imagine that you are standing somewhere, waiting for the bus for instance. Feel how you are standing. If your knees feel stiff, bend them a little so that they become softer in the joints.

But now it may feel as if the weight on your feet has shifted. Move your feet. That's better. But now one hip feels tight. Move it as well. And so on all the way through your body.

It's not that you're being fidgety; quite the opposite. All your muscles and joints are connected, either directly or through other muscles and joints. The change in the position of a joint will, through the muscles, affect the position of other joints. That's why

tensing the knee joint can bother the feet, hips, or back, and why loosening the tension in the knees gives you the impulse to loosen up in other places in your body.

As children, most of us were reminded to stand up straight. For a moment we straightened up and then we drooped over again. It was much too exhausting to sit so tensely in order to keep the back straight. That's just as well; it could have given you a headache to sit "correctly" for a long time.

A rounded back often starts at the hip joints. It is the position of the behind on the chair and the contact of the feet with the floor that should be changed. Instructions from others about what is right and wrong can be difficult to use appropriately. Only by paying attention to your own experience of your body will you be able to change something in a way that is right for you.

TENSING/RELAXING

In the previous chapter, I spoke about tensing and loosening up. Sit down and see if you are able to feel what I'm talking about.

Find a chair without armrests and with a level seat that you can sit in with your feet flat on the floor.

Lift one of your legs. Try to use just your thigh muscles so that your calf and foot hang heavily. In this position, your calf has what I call *gravity*.

Keep your leg up—tense it up to keep it there—and then let your leg fall with all its weight. Your foot should hit the floor with a thud; otherwise you didn't let go of the leg all at once.

How does your leg feel now? Have you released the tension?

Try again using the other leg. Were you able to let go of the leg all at once?

Do the same thing with your arms. Lift one arm to the side—hold it there by tensing it—then relax your wrist and let your hand hang down. Let the entire arm fall down heavily and notice what you feel. Does it feel different than the other arm, which you haven't lifted yet? Now try it with that arm. Were you able to let your hand hang down heavily?

These examples may seem simple, but most of us know from experience that some parts of the body are easier to relax than others, and that the different situations in which we find ourselves also influence how much we tense up.

Let's try something else you may remember from your childhood. Stand in a doorway. Lift your arms so that each hand touches the inside of the door frame and press against the frame. Press hard. Keep pressing as long as you can, but not so long that you feel pain anywhere. Move out of the doorway and let your arms hang down freely. If you don't actively hold your arms close to your body, they'll slowly move outward and upward.

This is because the tension you created in your muscles while you were pressing against the door frame doesn't disappear right away. The muscles are still working and are still tense. Only when your arms hang down freely alongside your body has the tension ceased.

This little game shows that we can tense our muscles without being conscious of it, and it illustrates that you can send a message to your muscles telling them to relax without your muscles obeying the order.

This is often how we experience tension. It can be difficult for us to tell our muscles to relax. For instance, you may sometimes draw your shoulders up to your ears. If you don't relax them after a while, and if you don't move them, the tension will become static. After a while, you'll stop noticing that your contracted shoulder muscles feel tense; you'll become accustomed to the feeling and will need a different type of impulse to re-experience the tension.

The tensions in the various parts of our bodies have innumerable causes, and I can't promise that you will be able to discover all of them by working with your body. Yet when you become aware of moments when you tense up, perhaps you'll notice what makes you do so and why. This will give you an opportunity to make changes in your daily situation.

Just as we may react with too much tension in the muscles, we may also react with too little. Such under-toned muscles often become overly stretched. If they surround a joint, their condition usually can be seen by observing the functioning of the joint. The joint's mobility is limited only by the structure of the bones, and if the muscles lack tension the joint can be moved too far. When this happens, the overly extended joint locks, resulting in bad coordination, and the movement loses its dynamic elasticity.

An example from my school days: I was praised for being flexible, but I was in fact too flexible. It turned out that first and foremost I couldn't throw a ball. This misery is called hyperextension, where the elbow joint may bend the wrong way. When I threw a ball, my elbow joint went out with a pop. The result was what we called a "sissy throw"—not much help if you're trying to throw someone out at third.

It's also possible to stand with overly extended knee joints, which bow backward. You are then hanging by your backside's muscles, which have to take over a part of the load-bearing function of the skeleton.

We can have overly stretched muscles all over the body. We often have a mixture of muscles with normal tension and muscles with too little tension. Try to notice whether you are supporting yourself by one or more joints, or whether you are locking any joints. I have mentioned the knees and elbows, but the hip joint can also be affected. In this case, by pulling in your behind you support yourself by the muscles on the front of the hips.

If you recognize any of this in yourself, you can occasionallly play with the feeling of being loose in the joints. But take care not to press to the limit any joints surrounded by overly stretched muscles while working with the movements in this book. It's better to limit them and to stay at the point where you can maintain the elasticity in your muscles.

BREATHING

Like everything else, breathing is influenced by our overall mood. Nervousness, anxiety, and pain make us breathe faster or momentarily stop breathing. If we are taking an exam, our breathing can take the form of a quick puffing in the upper chest without our having performed strenuous work. A fright will make us gasp for breath, sexual excitement makes us breathe faster; but if we are calm, our breathing is calm, too. Breathing is something that generally works by itself. If we try to think about it, it often becomes forced. You may want to give someone the impression you're asleep, for example, but it's almost impossible to imitate the calm breathing of sleep. After awhile, you force yourself so much to sound like you are lightly snoring that your breathing becomes uneven and strained.

In breathing, it is first and foremost the rib muscles and diaphragm that do the work. The diaphragm arches over our stomach and abdomen, stretching from the back all the way around to the rib cage. When the diaphragm is working, it moves up and down like a piston and helps pull air in and push it out again. As the diaphragm moves downward, it pushes our intestines beneath it, which then push against the skin of the abdomen, which expands to make more room. Actually, it's misleading to talk about breathing with the abdomen when it's the rib muscles and diaphragm that are doing the work, but I use the expression anyway because it is what is seen and felt.

Neither Rhea nor I use breathing exercises. Breathing is a part of all the movements we describe and inevitably has a rhythm in relation to what we are doing. A conscious effort to breathe deeply can help you get in touch with those spots that tense up, and make the feeling of interconnection more obvious. It is natural to breathe in when the body expands—in other words, when the movement opens up the body—and to breathe out when the movements seem to pull the body in. Yet breathing doesn't always work this way. Just as we often draw our shoulders up to our ears, we can tighten our breathing in the chest or squeeze it into a spot where it can't be seen or felt.

If you become aware that your breathing has stopped or become strained when performing a movement, it may be that the movement is too hard or complicated. It may also be that the movement is affecting something inside you that is uncomfortable or anxiety-provoking to deal with. Don't try to force your breath to be perfectly calm. If you do, it only means that you are tensing up against your own reactions or ignoring certain signals that perhaps you should be listening to. Respect your limits, and slowly and attentively see how far you can go with a movement without tensing against it.

In your daily life, try giving your breathing lots of room—for instance, when you wake up in the morning and stretch.

Let your chest and stomach expand and your mouth open so that the air can get right down to the bottom of your lungs. Afterward it can be blown out in a yawn, preferably a loud one.

On the whole, the various ways of breathing are full of sounds that we often suppress.

Try sighing with lots of air and sound. Fill your chest so it expands to all sides, imagine that you are breaking ropes that are wrapped around you, and then let out all the air again in one deep sigh.

Another thing you can do for your breathing is to make sure you are not constricting your abdomen with tight belts, narrow pants, etc. The lungs, intestines, muscles, and blood vessels function best when they are not contricted.

16

THE BODY'S AXES

In describing the body at rest and in motion, the expressions *length axis* and *cross axis* are helpful. These axes follow the anatomy of the body—in other words, the positions and functions of the bones and muscles—and combine the anatomical expressions for the planes of the body with the afspaending concept of ideal movements.

When we sit or stand within the body's axes, the skeleton's construction allows the bones to stabilize and support each other, and we use a minimum of muscle strength to maintain the position. When we're *out of axis*, the relative position of the bones is different. They're not supporting each other any longer, and the muscles must work in order to maintain the position.

Our bodies are *in axis* when our muscles are at rest without being shortened or lengthened, and when they are well coordinated. Based on this definition, the different ways our bodies are constructed will not affect our ability to be in axis. Yet there probably isn't a single person whose joints are in axis in every position. I, for one, have never met anyone who didn't have something or other that diverged from the ideal.

If I lie down in a basic supine position, we can observe where the axes would be placed if I were in axis, and where I am out of axis due to too much or too little tension.

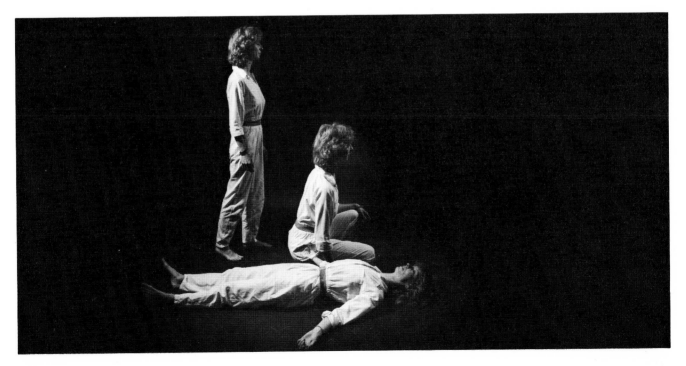

Basic Supine Position

Visualize the length axis as a straight line from the middle of the forehead down to the pubic bone, continuing down between the legs and feet. If I lie straight in relation to my length axis, it divides my body into two equal parts.

The cross axes lie perpendicular to the length axis. One goes from the hand through the arm and shoulder to the other arm and hand. The others go through the two hip joints, through the knees, and through the feet.

Are your various joints lying perpendicular to the length axis and thus straight in relation to each other?

If they are out of line, it means that some muscles are contracted while others are stretched beyond their resting point.

And now for the various joints.

We'll start at your feet. Are they resting on the heels and are your toes pointing up and out at an angle?

Are your legs positioned straight down from your hips, and are they turned out slightly from the hip joints so that your knees point in the same direction as your toes?

Are your shoulders positioned within the cross axis?

Well, they're not with me: they're drawn slightly above the cross axis. I must have tense—and as a result, shortened—muscles in that region.

Are your arms placed out from the body in a soft curve, resting on the mat? Are your wrists positioned in fairly small curves, and are your fingers slightly bent?

Are your neck and head positioned within the body's length axis, and is your head resting on the flat spot in the middle of the back of the head?

Roughly, these are the axes seen from above. If we view them from the side, we can see more clearly which muscles I'm able to relax, and which muscles are tense despite the supine position.

We'll begin again from the bottom.

Are your calves relaxed so that they're flattened out against the mat?

Your knee joints are relaxed when they are raised slightly above the mat. If you can place your entire hand underneath them as I can, then something

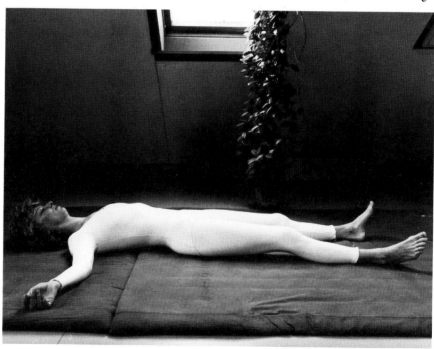

18

is too tight, and perhaps something else is too loose.

Are the upper parts of your thighs flattened out, and are the backs resting on the mat?

Do your hip bones fit with the lines of your body, or do they stick up? They do a little with me.

Is your behind flattened out against the mat?

If the small of your back is relaxed, you will be able to slip your hand underneath it.

You can't see breathing in a picture, but try to imagine where it's placed and what rhythm it has.

Are your shoulders resting on the mat?

Does the back of your neck make up a soft, small curve, with just enough room for a couple of fingers?

Is your face parallel with the mat, and does it feel relaxed?

It doesn't do any good to try to force yourself into positioning your body "correctly." You have to experiment with your body in order to find the position that is right for you.

There are a few simple movements that can be a great help for this.

Choose a room you like to be in and where you have enough space to lie down, stretch out, and place your arms out to the sides. Preferably, it should be quiet so that you can lie there undisturbed.

The mat you lie on should be fairly firm, and it shouldn't be so thick that you sink down into it. Lie down as much in the middle of the room as possible, and line yourself up in relation to the walls. This will make it easier for you to sense if you are lying in line with the axes of your body.

A leotard like the one shown in the pictures is actually not the best thing to wear, as it feels tight and will often be too cold. Rhea and I are wearing these outfits so that the lines of our bodies stand out clearly in the pictures. Something soft and warm that gives and isn't tight anywhere is best—for instance, a jogging suit or woolen leg-warmers, tights, and a sweatshirt.

Lie down on your back with your arms out to your sides and the palms of your hands facing upward if they can. Don't force them. Let your legs run straight down from your body. Give yourself time to lie there and relax, and notice your breathing.

Now try to feel all the way up through your body. Follow the description of the axes starting down by your feet and going up to your head. Give yourself plenty of time to notice every single part of your body. Do you feel where you are at rest, and where you can't relax?

Try to breathe deeply with your chest, with your diaphragm, and all the way down into your abdomen if possible. How are you lying?

Supine Stretching

I have spoken about having *gravity* in muscles that are at rest. Try now to maintain the feeling of the natural weight of your body when you stretch, despite the fact that you are using your muscles.

Start with one leg. Slowly stretch the back of your leg by lengthening it, foot flexed, along the floor, with your toes pointing straight up in the air. Let your leg remain heavy so that you use as little energy as possible. That way you avoid tensing up, and your muscles can be stretched slowly and steadily.

This is what I call *elastic stretching*.

Stop when you feel the tension increase in the front of your thigh.

If it's difficult to sense, it may help to place your hand on top of your thigh.

Stop stretching by releasing the tension in your entire leg all at once. Now try the same thing with your other leg.

Movements such as this one, where you use your muscles and then relax them, activate the venal pump, that is, the muscles' pressure on the veins, which helps to pump your blood back to your heart. This exercise can help if you are bothered by "tickling in the legs," an inner restlessness which occurs especially during the night.

After you have stretched both legs, let your arms slide along the floor up to your head.

While you are moving your arms, let your shoulder blades rotate with the movement so that you avoid lifting your shoulders up to your ears.

Now, using as little energy as possible in your heel and in your arm, stretch slowly, one side at a time, while you breathe in. Attempt to maintain the gravity in your back so that the small of your back becomes extended. If you arch up, stop stretching.

Can you avoid the hyperextension mentioned earlier by maintaining a slight curve in your elbow joint?

Now relax everything all at once while you exhale.

Feel whether there is a difference between the two sides of your body before you begin stretching the other side.

If two of you are working together, the stretch can be emphasized if the other person's hands are placed as shown in the picture and, without pushing, move upward in time with the stretching to emphasize the movement.

Legs Above Your Stomach

Slowly pull your legs up to a bent position and continue on up until they are above your stomach, with your knees still bent. Use your leg muscles as little as possible in order to activate an inner muscle called the *psoas*, which runs from the front of the hip through your back, and your lengthwise stomach muscles. When you use these muscles, you bring the hip bones and ribs closer together at the same time that your back lengthens against the floor and your stomach expands.

How are your legs doing hanging here?

You'll probably have to tense your

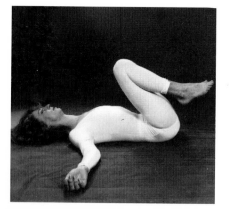

legs slightly so they don't fall to each side, but try to rest your entire body as much as possible.

With your legs above your stomach, shake your feet. Let them dangle up and down by the ankles, and then release your legs at the hip so that your feet hit the floor with a thump, still

with your knees bent. The thump tells you that you have let them fall without controlling the movement down to the floor.

Has any change taken place in the small of your back?

Your legs are now in what I call a *hook position*. Can you let them slide down from here to a lying position with the help of their own weight?

How are you lying now? Do you feel any difference from when you first began?

If something feels tight or in any way doesn't feel at rest, try supporting the area with a pillow. If you have an enlarged arch in the small of your back or the hollow of your knees, you can place a pillow under each knee. Not large pillows, but just enough for you to feel that they give support.

If your legs want to lean to the sides to such an extent that the outer part of your feet touch the mat, then make the

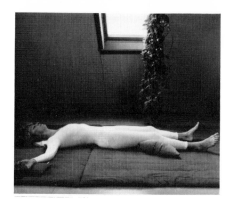

pillows thickest on the outer side of your knees. The pillows will then help your legs be in axis without your having to tense up in order to keep them there.

Does it feel good?

You can also support your position by placing pillows under your wrists and neck as shown in the picture. Be careful not to use pillows that are too large. They should only provide support and not exaggerate any arches you may have.

Once you have discovered how to give in to the force of gravity by paying careful attention to what your body tells you, as well as by using movements and pillows and letting your body rest by its own weight, you will have found your optimal resting position.

Give yourself time to feel and understand this gravity before you start on the afspaending and modern dance movements in this book. That way you'll have the best possible starting point and the opportunity to really feel how you use your body.

Basic Sitting Position

Look at the picture and notice the hip joint, where the thigh bone is connected to the pelvis. Try to find this joint on your own body.

From here your torso can move in relation to your legs. Moving from your hip joint gives you great freedom of movement in the sitting position.

Find a chair with a level seat that allows you to sit with your feet flat on the floor.

Sit down so that you are resting on your bottom.

A little higher than the lower edge of the buttocks, there are two bony projections of the pelvis called the seat bones (ischia). Place your hand under your buttocks and find them. When your pelvis is in axis, you are sitting on your seat bones. They are the center of your point of support.

Sit down with your thighs pointing straight out from your body and your feet flat on the floor.

Lift one of your thighs slowly with both hands until your foot is off the floor. Relax your leg so that you are carrying all of its weight with your arms.

Let your leg rest heavily in your hands with your foot hanging down.

Put your leg down and see whether you feel a difference. Now try this with the other leg.

Now, are your feet positioned? Is your weight equally divided between the front of your foot and your heel? If not, try to position your calves and feet vertically from your knees with your toes pointing straight ahead. Your legs are now in axis. How does it feel?

As mentioned previously, you can't change one part of your body without changes taking place somewhere else. For instance, when you are sitting, not only should your legs be relaxed but the angle in your hips should be just under 90 degrees if you are to find a restful balance.

Imagine that a plumb bob is hanging inside your body by a string attached to the middle of your head.

If you get out of axis by slouching, the string will slacken and the plumb bob will hit bottom. If you straighten up, yet lean in front of your length axis, the plumb bob will knock against the front of your body, and if you lean back, it will knock against the back. If you are sitting in axis, the string and plumb bob's line will go from the middle of your head straight down to the pubic bone. In order to find this balance, try a swaying motion around your length axis.

Arching Movements on a Chair

Start arching from your hip joints. Move your stomach slowly forward and stick your behind back so that you arch up from your hip joints by tilting your pelvis. Let the movement travel farther on through the small of your back to the point between your shoulder blades, up through your neck, until your neck and head follow the movement up and back.

Do you have a feeling of using your muscles without "tensing" them, so that you keep the feeling of gravity as much as possible?

If parts of your body are difficult to move smoothly, it may help to stop and breathe deeply.

Let the movement be slow enough that you have a chance to feel it running up from your hips through all the vertebrae in your back and neck as one long movement.

Don't arch any farther than feels good and don't lift your behind from the chair. The position may be strenuous, especially for your neck muscles, and also for your back, so don't hold it for too long.

In order to return to your starting position, first tilt your pelvis upward, and then pull yourself joint by joint up through your back and slowly on through the seven vertebrae in your neck so that your head comes up as the last section of a tall pillar.

Can you keep the movement slow

and steady so that you retain the feeling of gravity all the way up?

Rounding Movements on a Chair

The rounding of the back also starts at your hip joints.

With your behind placed in the same spot, let your hips tilt back so that the angle of your back to your thighs becomes greater than 90 degrees. Continue rounding up through your back by slowly releasing your muscles, finally letting your neck and head follow the movement forward.

Remain in this hanging position for a while. It may provide a nice stretch for your neck and back muscles.

Without using any energy, can you give even a little more with the help of your body's own weight?

Breathe deeply down to the small of your back so that you expand to all sides.

Now begin slowly to roll up to a position between a rounding and an arch; in other words, a relaxed straight back. First straighten your body up from

your hip joints and then let the movement run slowly on up through your body, ending with your head.

Now how are you sitting? Have you found the spot where your body is in restful balance?

Arm Movements

Let your arms hang down heavily by your sides, and give yourself time to sense whether they are relaxed.

Bring them slowly out to your sides while letting your shoulder blades turn freely toward your back as described in Basic Supine Position (page 18).

If your shoulder and neck muscles want to move up, don't force them down. Instead, do the movement more slowly and rotate your arms and the palms of your hands in a semicircle, turning them in while your arms are hanging alongside your body and bringing them forward until they're turned up when your hands are at shoulder height.

Loosening your elbows and rotating your arms and hands can help you

avoid pulling your shoulders up and maintain the gravity in your arms.

Remain sitting with your arms up and feel how much energy you have to use to keep them up. Can you relax a little without them falling down?

Now let them fall down with all their weight.

How do they feel?

After a while, you may get a tremendous desire to cross your legs and round your back. Don't feel forced to sit "correctly," but the more often you find this balance, the more familiar you'll become with the feeling, and eventually it will be one of the positions in which you'll choose to sit.

Don't think that we can sit still for eight hours straight, day in and day out, without any problems just because we sit properly.

Correct or incorrect posture, good or bad chair or table, we can discover what's best, but that doesn't change the fact that our bodies can suffer from staying in one position too long or from making the same movements over and over.

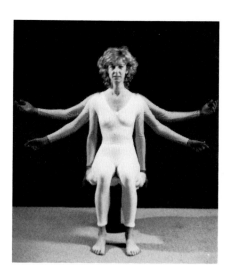

Basic Standing Position

In an attempt to find each individual's optimal standing position, we'll start with the feet because they are the basis for the balance of the entire body.

Stand with your feet just less than a foot's length apart, with the inner edges of your feet parallel and the tips of your toes pointing straight ahead. Tilt all your toes upward, spreading them at the same time. Then relax and curl your toes in under your feet, which will force you to stand on the outer edge of your feet.

What happens to the tension in your legs?

Spread your toes again, relax them, and finish up by shaking your feet.

How do your feet feel now?

Standing Pendulum

Imagine that your feet have deep roots, and that your body is a long, straight trunk. Your ankle is the one joint that can be moved, from which you can bend forward or backward. Start by leaning forward just as far as you can without raising your heels and tearing up some of the roots.

How is the tension in your feet and legs?

Return to the starting position and lean backward, watching out for your roots. Where are you tensing now?

Lean forward again, and this time try to release some of the tension without losing your balance.

Where do you keep tensing, and where do you stretch?

Try the same thing while leaning backward.

Continue to swing back and forth while you make the movement smaller and smaller. Notice how you move your weight and vary the tension in your muscles.

Stop at the point where you are standing with the least possible tension in your legs. Try again to feel the plumb bob hanging in your body. Does it hang so that it points down toward the center of the arches of your feet?

Accordion

Maintain the feeling that your feet are well planted in the ground. Bend at the ankles, knees, and hips, with your knees pointed forward and your behind pulled in.

Try bobbing up and down by increasing and decreasing the bending in your joints so that you fold like an accordion.

Bob a little more and try to point your knees straight out over your toes. Rise up slowly and stop just before your knees and hip joints lock.

If you are used to stretching your joints completely to their limits, this movement may give you the strange feeling that you have rubber knees and that your behind is sticking out. It may be tough to walk around like this, but try every once in a while to play with the feeling of loose joints.

Now that you're standing with your knees and hips in a comfortable position, you have an opportunity to find the balance in your back.

Roll Down from Standing Up

The topmost vertebra in the neck is higher up than you might imagine. Using your fingers, find a bump at the bottom of the back of your head, just below the level of the middle of your ears. This is where your vertebrae begin.

Let your head bend forward from this point, placing your chin against the front of your throat. Then let the weight of your head pull you slowly downward, vertebra by vertebra.

We have seven neck vertebrae, which together can make up a soft curve instead of a straight line. Roll on downward and let your back's vertebrae be a part of the movement.

When you feel like it, release your knees and hips, and bend them so that you don't tense up to keep your balance. Let your arms and shoulders hang heavily. Do you feel how your muscles are connected?

The first few times you do this I wouldn't advise rolling farther down than where you can look at your stomach. In any case, you should never roll farther down than where it feels good.

It's not a matter of reaching the floor, but of moving the numerous joints in your neck and back by using your body's own weight, and feeling the stretch that your body's weight gives to your muscles.

Roll slowly up again by pulling yourself up from your hips, joint by joint through the small of your back, then your back and neck, and finally your head.

See if you can let your arms and shoulders be passive in the entire upward movement and just follow along.

How are you standing now? Do you feel a difference between before and after the movement?

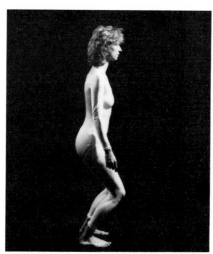

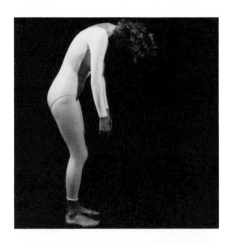

Standing Stretches

Finally, try the same movements with your arms and legs that you did while sitting on a chair. Give yourself time to feel the heaviness in your arms.

If there are two of you, your friend can slowly lift your upper arm outward, hold it a little, and then let go. Both of you will be able to tell whether you controlled your arm or let it hang by its own weight.

Try again with your other arm.

Now raise your arms up, letting the palms of your hands rotate forward and then upward as your arms reach shoulder level and continue up over your head.

If you raise your shoulders, your friend can follow your shoulder blades' rotation and help you keep the movement against your back instead of up toward your ears.

Maintain a soft curve in your elbow joints and bring your arms farther up over your head, stopping just before they are all the way up. If you bring your arms completely up and lock your elbow joints, your muscles can't give much more.

Stretch your whole body one arm at a time. Try to see whether you can make the stretch run down your back without arching the small of your back. Use your elasticity instead of force, and stretch all the way out to your fingers.

Release the stretch by letting your arms get heavy and collapse by your sides. Did you feel how you are connected?

Pillows in Rest Positions

We've just discussed the three positions—lying, sitting, and standing—that with thousands of variations we use every day of our lives. You can easily apply what you have just tried to everyday positions to avoid discomfort and find the best possible balance between tension and relaxation.

There is one more basic position—prone, lying on your stomach face down—which you will use in certain movements. I won't analyze it the way I did with the three other, but I will give you some examples of how you can use pillows to make this position more comfortable.

If you are lying flat on your stomach with your head to one side, your neck and shoulder muscles may be pulled and your chest pressed against the floor. Try laying a pillow underneath

the shoulder toward which your head is turned. If this doesn't help enough, then use still another pillow and move them around until you're lying comfortably.

Your ankle and knee joints may also feel tight in this position, and this is relieved by placing small pillows under your ankles.

In positions where you are lying on your side, you can support yourself with a pillow underneath the shoulder and another large one under the upper bent leg.

When you're sitting on a dining-room chair, lounge chair, or in a car, you can use pillows under your buttocks if the seat is too low. Pillows behind your back may help if the seat is too deep, or if the back of the seat or chair isn't properly contoured.

We don't become stronger or more flexible by supporting our bodies with pillows all over the place. But pillows can provide an opportunity for a rest in parts of the body that are otherwise tense a great deal of the time.

Pillows can also help us get closer to the optimal axes where muscles and joints aren't twisted, overly stretched, or pressed together. This way you have an opportunity to work *with* rather than *against* gravity. Eventually, lying, sitting, and standing in balance can lead to your changing your way of moving without thinking about it, quite simply because being in balance feels good.

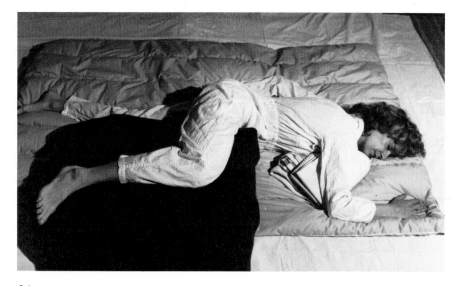

How Do You Use the Movements?

I advise you to work with the movements in the first section until you know them so well that you don't need to refer to the book or think too much about what to do.

When you have reached that point, you can begin to work with the movements in the following section, which build upon what you have already done.

The sitting movements in the third section and the walking and feet movements, however, needn't wait until you know the other movements.

Use the movements as often as you like, but don't turn them into an exercise program where you keep on until you are tired or sore. They're not any more effective when repeated ad infinitum.

The purpose of the movements is to make you conscious of how you use your body through experiencing how your body is connected, and by sensing how its various parts function. To achieve this you must have patience and work slowly in order to give yourself time to feel what is happening.

Your muscles will also need time to relax to allow the passive stretches to have an effect on them. This in turn will make it easier to let go of more tension and to become even more aware of how your body works.

Working with your body in this way involves your entire self. Some of the movements may affect you in ways you didn't expect. Take what you feel as something your body is telling you, something you can learn from.

If you feel that you are tensing up, holding your breath, or becoming uncomfortable, then be extra attentive to yourself and try to make the movement smaller so that you aren't forcing yourself. The discomfort you feel may be a sign that you are unconsciously resisting.

Changing your body movements this way doesn't have to make you feel un-comfortable, but it may, because there's a connection between your state of mind and what you experience in working with afspaending.

Movements 1

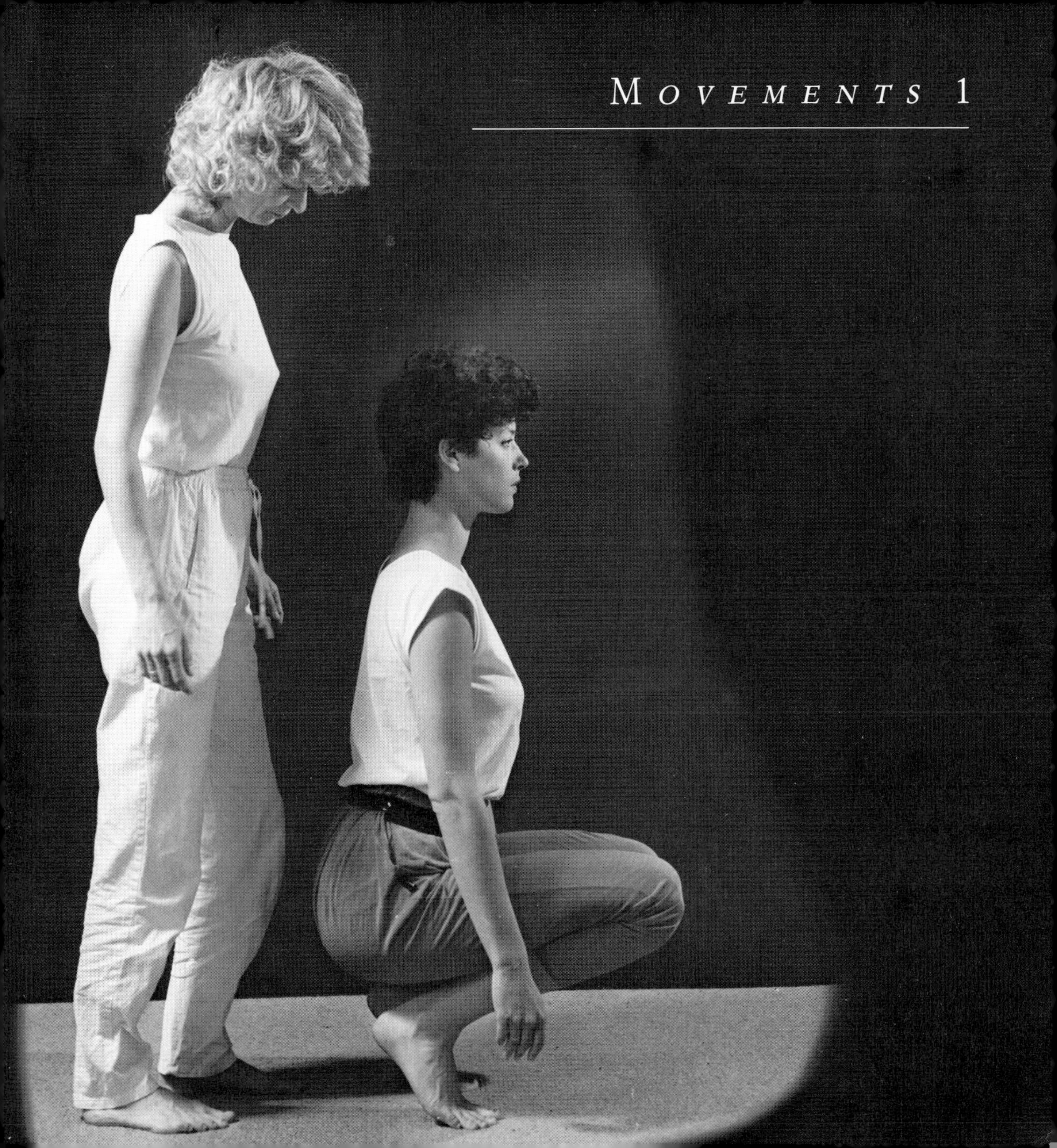

Basic Lying-Down Movements

Lie down on your back on a mat like the one you used in Basic Supine Position (see page 18), and start off with some of the movements that helped you to relax.

Give yourself plenty of time.

Stretch Up to Your Heels

Pull your bent legs up over your stomach. As you did before, try to let your legs become heavy and use your psoas and stomach muscles in the movement. Can you feel them?

Find the position where you use the least amount of energy to keep your legs hanging and then grasp them just below your knees with your hands.

Pull your legs down carefully toward your stomach while keeping them aligned with the length axis, so that the distance between your knees and your feet is just a little less than the width of your hips. Don't pull them past the point where you can keep your behind on the floor.

Let go of your knees and let them pop up again without letting your feet drop to the floor.

How is your back positioned now?

If your behind is raised from the mat, you can let your feet drop a bit so that your back and sacrum rest as one long unit against the floor.

Shake your feet up and down. Try to relax them so that they loosen completely. Don't shake them from side to side, since ankle joints are often a little too loose when moved sideways.

Release the weight of your legs all at once, letting them drop down onto the floor with your feet in a bent position.

As before, the thump tells you whether or not you let go of your legs all at once.

Are your legs and feet resting comfortably now?

Lift one leg slowly upward, going no farther than the point where your thighs are still parallel to each other. Stop before the position feels too tight or if you sense that you are tensing up other places in your body. Find the angle that fits you best.

Now try to draw a circle with the tips of your toes. Move them all the way around, first in one direction, then in the other. Use as little muscle strength as possible.

Is there freedom of movement in the joint?

Next, bend your ankle so that your foot is flexed and you're stretching the back of your leg. Can you concentrate on the feeling of gravity in the muscles of the back of your leg so that they slowly and steadily stretch out?

How far can you feel the stretching?

Let go of the stretching and at the same time bend your knee and lower your leg over your stomach and then down, placing your foot flat on the floor.

Do you feel a difference between your legs? What about the contact the soles of your feet have with the mat?

Repeat this movement with your other leg.

These stretches also help your venal pump, which I mentioned in Basic Supine Position (page 18), and they can also relieve restlessness in your legs.

If your foot-to-floor contact isn't good, then move your feet around a little until you find the spot where the pressure you feel against the floor is fairly evenly divided between the front of your foot and your heel.

The muscles you are now going to work with are the so-called "seat muscles" and the pelvic floor. The seat muscles are the back of your hips and buttocks, as well as some lesser muscles. The pelvic floor is another term for the musculature stretching forward from the rectum to the vagina or penis and up to the stomach muscles, as well as many small muscles in your abdomen. These groups of muscles as well as the stomach muscles are important for keeping your abdominal organs—the stomach, intestines, bladder, and for women the uterus—in place. If the muscles are tense, they can tighten up around the internal organs, which can cause discomfort and pain, and if the muscles are too slack, they don't give the necessary support. For women, this can lead to a prolapsed uterus or a vagina that has lost its tone. If either of these has happened, don't despair. You can actually raise up your uterus and tighten your vagina by exercising the muscles of your pelvic floor. Loss of urinary control can also be helped through working with these muscles.

Moving Your Pelvis with Your Stomach

Lie down again with your legs bent and your feet flat on the floor. Are your feet positioned well? Try to contract your stomach muscles without lifting your legs. Do this by reducing the distance between your pubic bone and ribs, which in turn will bring the small of your back closer to the floor and make your stomach harder.

Release any tension that has accumulated and breathe calmly and deeply a

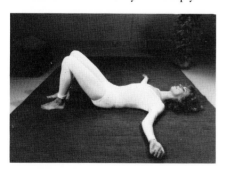

few times.

If you find this difficult, then imagine that you are pushing something inside your stomach downward toward the floor.

Try again. Notice this time how your pelvis moves when the small of your back approaches the floor, and what happens when you release the tension.

Do the movement a few times using your own or a friend's hands to emphasize the contraction of the stomach. When you work with the movement several times in a row, remember to relax completely between movements and to breathe deeply with your stomach.

Moving Your Pelvis with Your Buttocks

Try now to rock your pelvis in the same way by squeezing your buttocks together.

Tighten your buttocks slowly, keep them there, and then release the tension.

What happened to your pelvis and the small of your back? Did they make the same movement as before?

As you probably noticed, it was impossible to use only your buttocks, as the movement involves other muscles as well. Yet it is possible to concentrate

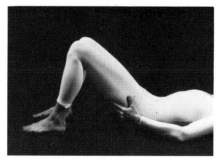

on various muscle groups.

Try again. Place your hands on your buttocks and feel how you press them together when you tighten them, and how they become completely soft when you let go.

Concentrate next on your pelvic floor and your buttocks. See whether you can relax the rest of your body while you are working on the movement.

Start by tightening your buttocks and letting the tension run from your anus to your vagina or penis, so that the entire pelvic floor is included in the movement. It may be difficult to use these muscles. Try several times.

Can you let the tension spread so that it becomes one movement, moving your pelvis along with it?

Moving Your Pelvis with the Pelvic Floor and Stomach

Now you are going to try to make the pelvic floor and your stomach muscles work together.

Start by contracting the pelvic floor. Then try to let the contraction spread into your abdomen and the lower stomach muscles and get a feeling of pushing your inner organs farther up toward your diaphragm.

Did your pelvis move?

Let go of the tension and breathe

deeply before you try again. Can you make your muscles work together in pushing upward?

Relax again, rest awhile, and give in to your breathing so that you expand all the way down to your abdomen and pelvis.

In these and the following movements, it will probably feel most natural to let the movement take place as you exhale, because the contraction helps to push the air out. Try it the other way around as well. I find it feels odd.

Moving Your Pelvis Starting from Your Legs

Bend your knees, place your feet flat on the floor, and start the movement from here without moving them. Try to feel as if there is energy running up through your legs to your hips that thrusts your feet against the floor. Your pelvis should move in such a way as to even out the angle between your thighs and hips so that the small of your back is flatter on the floor.

Try to let your pelvis hang by your legs so that you only use a bit of energy in your legs. Let go and let your pelvis move back again.

Try once more, and feel whether you can do the movement without tightening your stomach or diaphragm.

If you can breathe with your stomach while the small of your back is on the floor, your stomach can't be all that tense.

Let go of your legs and let your feet slide along the floor, pulling your legs along to a lying position. Did you feel how these muscles work, and could you relax them when they didn't need to work?

Finish off by stretching, either any way

you like or according to the stretches described in Basic Supine Position (page 18).

It is a good idea to get into the habit of stretching especially when you have been sitting or lying quietly and suddenly have to get up and start moving again. It will get your blood circulation going and force you to breathe deeply so that you take in lots of oxygen.

To sit up easily from a lying position, roll on your side and curl yourself up a little before using your arms to push yourself up. This way you avoid using your shoulders to pull yourself up.

How are you feeling now?

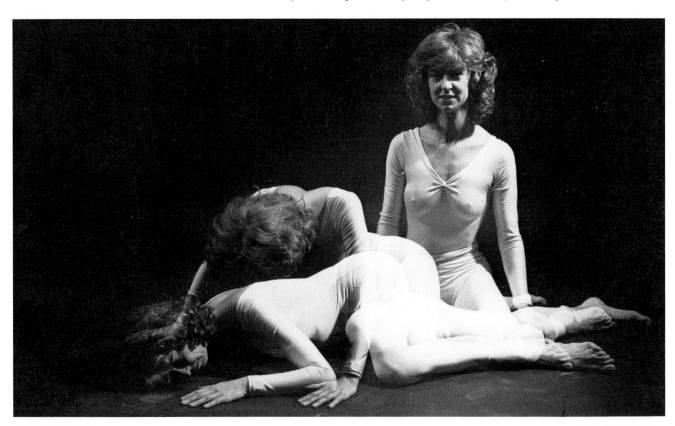

Basic Sitting Movements

Did you ever sit in gym class in school with your legs stretched out, trying to touch your toes with your fingers?

Impossible! most of us in my class said.

If we had started by pulling our pelvis back so we were sitting on the bottom of our buttocks instead of their back, then we would in fact have stood a chance.

Try these two starting positions

yourself, sitting on a pillow if it feels comfortable. It's not guaranteed that you'll reach your toes, but you'll be in a position to move your hip joints, and that's what's most important.

In the following movements, concentrate on moving from the hip.

Sitting Flower

Bend your legs and let your knees fall to each side with the soles of your feet touching each other.

Can you find the two bony projections, the sit bones, which you found in the Basic Sitting Position (page 21)?

Place your hands underneath your buttocks with your fingers in front of the sit bones and pull back one buttock at a time. If there are two or more of you, you can help each other by gently pulling the behind backward.

When you are sitting up on your sit bones, your hips are at an angle to your legs that allows freedom of movement in the hip joint. It is far less important how much your knees swing upward.

If you can't sit without straining your back, then place a pillow under your behind.

Now, with a straight back, try to rock slightly back and forth starting from your hip joints. Can you do it without moving the small of your back? If it becomes uncomfortably tight, you should save the movement for later, and you can try the following movement instead, which involves working with some of the same muscles.

When you have found the spot where you can move your hip joint without it hurting, tilt forward with a straight back. Come as far forward as you can without bending your back or straining

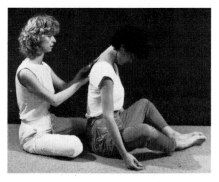

yourself, and then relax by letting the small of your back curve, and letting your back, neck, and head follow the movement forward. Stay here awhile without forcing yourself farther down, letting your body's own weight work for you.

Can you breathe deeply so that you expand the floor of your pelvis? How does the stretch in your back feel? Do you feel a stretch anywhere else?

Roll up by first tilting your hips slightly backward and upward. If there are two of you, the feeling can be enhanced if your partner's hands are placed firmly at the very bottom of your back to remind you that the pull should come from there. Continue to roll up slowly through your back, placing your spine and neck's vertebrae up on top of each other one by one.

Can you let your arms, shoulders, and the part of your back which you haven't pulled up yet hang heavily?

Your partner's hands can follow the movement along your spine so that you can feel more easily whether there are places where you are tensing up or where you miss the rolling movement.

Try again to tilt from your hips. Has a change taken place?

Half-Flower

Despite what its name suggests, this movement isn't easier than the previous one, but it may help you sit without pain.

Extend one of your legs straight ahead and bend the other so that the

34

continuing up through your back to your head. Don't forget to breathe, stopping every once in a while to feel if by breathing deeply you can rely more on gravity, and then continue up.

You can use your friend's hands in the same way as in the previous movement.

Shift legs, give yourself time to find your starting position, and repeat the movement with your other leg extended.

sole of the foot on the bent leg touches the knee on your straight leg. Use a pillow under the extended knee and your behind if this gives you more freedom of movement. Again, the most important thing is that you find the spot where you sit best, and from which you can move your hip joint.

Fall forward with a straight back over the extended leg. Don't force yourself down. When you feel that you can't come any farther without tensing or pressing, let your body hang down over your leg. Stay here awhile, and breathe deeply over the small of your back.

Feel the connection from your heel all the way up to your head. Are there any places where you can let gravity work so that you give a little?

Roll up from your hips as before,

Heel-Sitting Pendulum

You should be very careful with this movement if you have a bad knee; stop immediately if it hurts at all.

Sit with your legs folded underneath you, your behind resting against the soles of your feet, and lean forward so your behind is as far back as it can be.

Place a pillow between your thighs and calves if it is uncomfortable to have your legs bent so much. You can also place a pillow under your ankles if they feel too stretched. Try to find a position where you feel comfortable.

How are you sitting now? Think about the plumb bob in your body. Are you now resting in balance? If you want, you can arch and round as you did in the Basic Sitting Position (page 21). Try to feel the length axis and

then arch around it. This way you can find the balance in your body, and you don't need to tighten your thighs, buttocks, and stomach in order not to fall.

Now rock back and forth from your hip joints. Keep your back long and straight, and see how big the swings are that you can make with your torso.

Can you feel how the movement originates from your hip joints?

Try to pull your behind underneath you. Now what happens with the movement?

What I think will happen is that you won't be able to move your hip joint anymore. You'll only be able to move forward from your waist, and the movement will become smaller and more strenuous.

If this is the first time you are working with these movements and your legs feel sore, bring them in front of your body and shake them before you get up. When you know the movements better, and it's easier to find your starting position for them, continue with the following.

The Cat

Start in the same position as the last movement and place your hands on

your thighs. Tilt forward with a straight back from your hip joints, sliding your hands forward so that they end up on the floor in front of your knees. Stop here and find a good contact between the palms of your hands and the floor. Try to avoid hanging by your shoulders, and maintain the soft curve at your elbow joints. Now slide forward on your hands using your body's weight. Let your behind tilt up

from your heels and follow the movement forward.

Stop once in a while to feel whether you're getting an overall stretch from your hands to your buttocks. If it's difficult, slide back a little and try to draw your shoulder blades down your back.

Did you feel the connection?

Stretch forward again slowly, no farther than where you still have most of your weight on your lower legs.

Can you sway a little like a tightened string and feel how the stretching spreads? Breathe deeply and let go of the stretch while you let yourself slide down toward the floor.

Lie down, curl up slightly with your forehead against the floor and your arms at your sides, and let a deep breath make you expand the small of your back and your behind before you pull yourself up.

continue the rolling movement up with the last part of your back.

Could you feel the connection from the tip of your spine to your hands?

It is a difficult movement that involves the coordination of your entire body. If you observe a cat or dog stretching, you'll see how the movement unfolds into one long stretch.

Start with your pelvis, which in a long, steady movement pulls your back up vertebra by vertebra, ending with your head. Try to let your arms and shoulders passively follow along.

Can you feel the weight of your body?

The Role of the Helper

If you want to help someone else with the movement, place your hands on your partner's behind and give yourself time to feel that your hands are resting with their own weight. In order to help get the upward movement to start from the hips, press down lightly as if you wanted to smooth the buttocks down toward the floor, and then follow the movement joint by joint up the spine.

Try to see whether by following the neck's seven vertebrae with your fingers you can help give the feeling that the

vertebrae can be stacked on top of each other joint by joint.

Variation of the Cat

When you have reached the point where you were lying and feeling how you can sway like a string, try to come back up with your torso while your arms are stretched forward.

Move your pelvis in toward your heels to curve the small of your back.

Gradually relax your body, and let your seat come all the way down on your heels. Use your body's gravity as much as you can, and roll your hips and the small of your back backward while you let go of the stretch and lift your hands from the floor.

Stay sitting at this point awhile and feel whether your shoulders, arms, and head are hanging heavily, and then

Stretch Forward and Breathe

In the same way as before, take time to find your balance and the proper freedom of movement in your hips.

Then fall forward with a straight back to lie with your stomach against your thighs. Let go completely so that you are lying with the weight of your entire body against your thighs and breathe deeply with your stomach, letting it spread out to your pelvis.

Lie here as long as it feels good, and then roll up as before.

To stand up, you can pull yourself up on your knees with the help of your thigh muscles. Tilt back a little from your hip joints so that the small of your back curves backward. Then try to pull yourself up by using the muscles on the front of your thighs.

37

Can you avoid drawing your shoulders upward?

Place one foot firmly on the floor. Place your weight on it, push up so you come to a standing position, and finish by stretching.

Try this every so often. It is good practice in not using your shoulders for everything, and a beautiful, flowing way to rise up.

Basic Standing Movements

As in the lying and sitting positions, first find your best starting position. Stand with just under a foot length's distance between your knees and feet and with feet as parallel as possible without feeling awkward.

Curl and spread your toes and sway back and forth until you find your balance.

Rotate from Your Ankle Joint

Imagine again that your feet have roots and try to draw a circle with your head while you let your body become a long, straight trunk which can be moved only from the ankle. Turn slowly around in circles not greater than where you can keep your feet completely on the floor.

Make the circles smaller and smaller while you feel how the weight on your feet shifts with the movement.

Turn the other way as well. What happens to the tension in your legs?

Make the circles smaller and smaller again until you stop at the point where you feel that the weight is evenly distributed over both feet, perhaps a little more on the front part of the feet than the back.

How are you standing now?

You will later feel in the modern dance movements how important foot contact and balance are in order to be able to move your body freely. Try to play with the feeling in various situations—for instance, while traveling in a bus or train. If you maintain foot contact and follow the ground's movements with your body instead of tensing against it, it'll take quite a lot to knock you over.

The Carousel

Shake your feet and find your roots again. Now your trunk can twist around itself without bending to the sides, as your joints become soft again. Let your arms hang heavily down by your sides and start twisting your body first one way and then the other.

For once the movement should be quick rather than slow. Let your arms swing with it. Twist yourself around your length axis while you try to relax your arms and hands; let them fly up-

ward and outward, following the movement.

Stop your body suddenly without braking your arms' movement. If you can retain the gravity in your arms, they will continue in smaller and smaller swings until the energy from the movement is used up. How did it feel?

This movement is good if you have difficulty letting your arms, hands, and shoulders relax by their own weight.

Dynamic Arm-Stretching to the Sides

Bring your arms out to your sides. Try to see whether you can use the movements learned in Basic Standing Position (page 23) and Basic Sitting Position (page 21) so that your arms, hands, and shoulder blades follow the movement, and your elbows remain slightly bent.

If there are two of you, your partner's hands placed as before can help you keep your shoulders down.

Stop when your hands are at shoulder height; if your elbows are still soft, they'll be slightly below shoulder height.

Let your partner, who's standing behind you, hold you by your wrists. Hold up your own arms at first, but when you have good contact with each other, try to relax your arms and shoulders completely. Your friend will hold your arms in the same position, which gives you a chance to get rid of tension, not only in your arms but also in any other places where you have tensed up.

When your partner lets go of your wrists, try to use the least possible amount of energy to regain control of your arms.

Do you feel a difference? If you are working alone, give yourself time to feel whether there are any places where you can get rid of tension without your arms falling down, although it's all right if they drop a little.

Now stretch to the side with one arm at a time, keeping your elbows softly curved so you don't block the stretch. The stretch should be long and steady so that it travels from your arms past your shoulders, and around between your shoulder blades.

It helps to have a hand placed be-

Javanese Variation

After having stretched all the way out to your fingertips, now try bending your wrists up so that the palms of your hands point out to the sides and then stretch out one arm at a time.

This stretches muscles that are otherwise difficult to get in touch with.

Can you feel how you are connected all the way out to your fingers?

Dynamic Forward Arm-Stretching

Bend your arms slightly and bring them up and forward with the palms of your hands facing each other. When your hands are slightly below shoulder height, try to let go of some of the tension in your shoulders and arms. Then stretch forward one arm at a time all the way to your fingertips; don't worry if your arms are not quite parallel.

tween your spine and shoulder blade, to follow the movement outward.

If it is difficult to keep your shoulders down and back, then let the stretch become smaller and stay at the point where you can stretch without tensing up.

It also helps to have a hand placed on each of your shoulders.

Stretch out, shifting from one arm to the other, all the way out to your fingertips. Repeat this several times, and then let your arms fall down heavily to your sides.

Try to do the movement again as one long stretch that goes all the way around your shoulders to the muscles between your shoulder blades. What happens then to your shoulders and elbows?

If you have a partner with you, you can help each other the same way you have in the previous movements. It isn't easy to get all these muscles working together. Just being able to feel which muscles do what can be difficult. So don't get frustrated because you don't succeed at first.

Once you have felt the connection between your arms, shoulder blades, and back, you can transfer this feeling to all kinds of everyday movements. Stretch you arm while at the same time bending your hip joint so that your behind points backward. You'll discover that you can reach quite far.

When you work with the modern dance movements in the second part of the book, try to use what you have learned from working with these movements. The dance movements will be less of a strain and flow more easily.

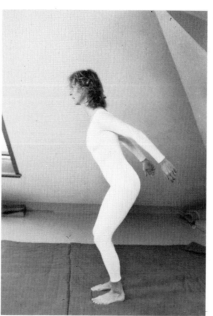

The Ski Movement

Let's take a ski run. It can't be done without a good connection to the ground. If your feet are tired, shake them a few times, and then place them about a foot apart, pointing straight ahead. If your toes point out, then your skis will each slide in a different direction.

Do you remember the accordion movement (page 24)? Try it again, bending your knees and hips as if your body were made up of equal parts that can fold together at your joints. Let

your behind point down and back at a slant and your knees point straight ahead so that they block your view of your toes.

Rock up and down—a little faster—and let your arms loosen up. Do they swing back and forth by themselves?

Swing faster, pushing down from your feet, and if your arms don't go

along with the movement in great big swings then help them along and try again to move in such a way that they swing on their own.

Speed up. Does your breathing follow the rhythm of the swinging?

When your ski run has been long enough, end the swinging by throwing your arms up over your head and stretch.

How do you feel now?

If you feel refreshed, then use this new energy; if you are tired, then rest a bit.

I'd like to emphasize that it isn't better to be either tired or refreshed. What's important is that you notice how you feel and pay attention to it.

If you need to rest, you can try lying down as shown in the picture.

Legs on a Big Pillow

Lying in this position is therapeutic in itself, because it gives the muscles in the small of your back a chance to rest against a mat without being stretched too much, which they would be if you were to sit in a chair with your back rounded.

The position is also good if you have a tendency to get swollen legs or varicose veins, because your legs are raised above heart level, and it's easier for your blood to flow back to your heart.

You can use whatever you want, a chair, large pillows, or layers of blankets. What's important is that they are of the right size, not quite as high as your thighs are long, and that your legs are comfortable.

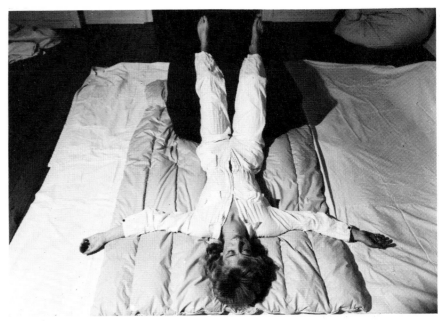

When you lie with your legs up on the pillows, feel whether they are lying straight in relation to your length axis. Also feel whether your right and left knees and your hip joints are equally bent.

Pull your legs up over your stomach so that the small of your back is pressed down on the floor and place them back on the pillow. Is your back at rest now?

If the angle between your hips and your thighs is too small, then move a little bit away from the pillow. You shouldn't feel bunched up.

How are you lying now? Feel your body all the way from your feet, your calves, your knees, up through your trunk, out to your arms and hands, and up to your neck, jaw, and eyes. Try to relax totally.

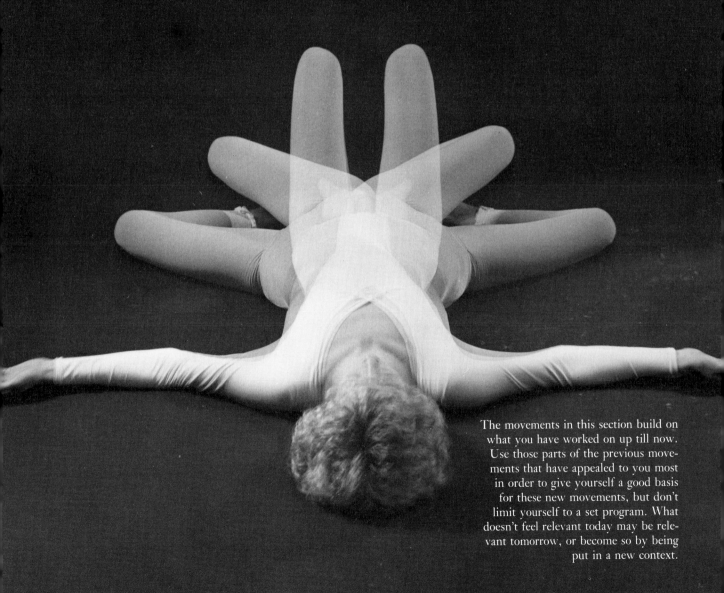

The movements in this section build on what you have worked on up till now. Use those parts of the previous movements that have appealed to you most in order to give yourself a good basis for these new movements, but don't limit yourself to a set program. What doesn't feel relevant today may be relevant tomorrow, or become so by being put in a new context.

Lying Movements

Lie on your back and pull your legs up over your stomach. Try this time to avoid pulling with the muscles in your shoulders and chest.

Do your shoulders remain down, resting against the mat?

Lying Flower

Let your feet drop down flat on the floor. Are they in a firm position?

Let go at your hips so that your knees slide out to the side and the soles of your feet touch each other. Lie like

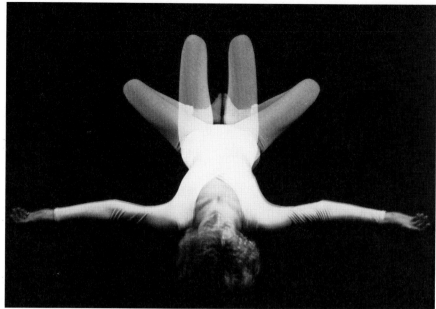

this for a while, letting the weight of your legs stretch your muscles, and try to breathe all the way down to your abdomen. Do you feel how you are connected?

If the position stretches your joints so much that it is uncomfortable, you can let one leg slide, knee bent, so that your other foot touches your knee. Now the stretch is taking place one side at a time; is that better?

Lie in the same way and let the weight of your body work for you. Do your muscles want to give?

Pull both legs up to a bent position; lie awhile and repeat the movement with your other leg bent out to the side.

You shouldn't lie like this too long; it can make you sore.

Let both legs slide down to a parallel position and stretch.

When working with modern dance in the second part of this book, you will find that many movements involve the muscles that you have stretched here. If the stretches in the modern dance section are too strenuous, use these movements to get a sense of what your limits are, to see how far you can go without tensing up, and to stretch your muscles passively so that they become more elastic.

Save the next movement for another time if you have become sore or tired. If not, once again pull your legs up over your stomach.

It may seem strange to extend your legs after each movement, only to raise them again for the next one. This is important because it gives you a chance to relax your entire body. In addition, raising and lowering your legs is a movement that strengthens your stomach muscles.

If your stomach muscles are too weak (which often happens when one is engaged in sedentary work), other parts of your body will have to compensate for this weakness in ways that are inappropriate.

While practicing modern dance movements, you will clearly feel the importance of your stomach's strength and elasticity.

Hip Swing

Bend both knees so that your feet are flat on the floor, and then let both knees fall over, leaning to one side. Can you keep your shoulders on the floor without having to tense up?

If your upper leg wants to swing out or up, place a hand on your knee to keep it down; this can also emphasize

the stretch around your hips. Try in this position to breathe deeply with your stomach. This helps you to let go if you are tense anywhere, and to check if you are holding back with your stomach.

Pull your legs up with the help of your stomach muscles so that your feet are flat on the floor again. If you use these muscles, the small of your back will be lying against the floor. Do the movement slowly and steadily so that you have time to feel which muscles you are using and how they work.

Let your knees fall over to the other side and lie there while you let the weight of your legs stretch your muscles.

Chaplin

You are now going to concentrate on your stomach muscles. The ones you are going to use in this movement go off diagonally from your length axis, and make it possible for you to use your stomach for asymmetric movements.

With one hand on your side so you can feel what you are doing with your muscles, and without pushing your legs, try using your stomach muscles to hike up the edge of your hip bone to-

ward your ribs on the same side.

Can you get in touch with the muscles? What about the muscles on the other side; can you avoid using them?

Try to contract the muscles on the other side. Concentrate now on your back. If it is relaxed, the small of your back will approach the mat when you pull with your stomach.

Try this several times. Can you feel how your muscles are working?

As in the other movements discussed so far, you should always give yourself time after this one to relax your stomach muscles. Relaxing the tension in your muscles is just as important as working with them. It's the alternation between tension and relaxation that gives them elasticity.

The Worm

This movement demands good foot contact and is a continuation of the three pelvis moves on page 31. I sug-

gest you work with them first.

Begin the movement by pushing your pelvis up with your feet, letting the energy travel up through your legs to your pelvis, which tilts up, and

keeping the small of your back on the floor.

Continue the movement by slowly pulling your pelvis upward so that the vertebrae in the small of your back and then in the rest of your back are pulled, leaving the mat one by one.

Stop occasionally and breathe deeply with your stomach. Let it puff out like a balloon being filled up with air.

Give yourself time to feel how your muscles work, and stop before it becomes strenuous. At any rate don't roll up any farther than the point where you are resting on the top part of your shoulder blades.

Try to stretch out the front of your hips a little so that your legs and hips become one long, straight line. Stay here for a while. Can you relax your stomach and buttocks? Where and how far do you then feel the stretch?

Roll slowly down again, letting go

vertebra by vertebra, beginning at your shoulders. Stop if there are difficult spots and breathe deeply to expand them.

When you come to the small of your back, press your stomach toward your back, and roll the small of your back down before your pelvis hits the floor.

Let you legs slide down and rest a little. How are you feeling now? Could you feel your back's mobility?

Next time you do the movement, feel whether your neck and shoulders are relaxed enough so that your head and arms are allowed to passively follow the movement.

Working with a Partner

If there are two of you, you can help each other. After you have rolled up, have your partner hold your knees and carefully pull them a little upward.

That way you can straighten out your hip joints and stretch the front of your body.

As you roll down, it helps to have a hand under your spine to follow the movement of your joints. Finally, it helps to have a hand under your behind to support it until you have placed the small of your back on the floor. The hand should offer gentle support but shouldn't resist your movement.

When giving support during the movements, the partner should always be attentive to the other person's movements and never try to force anything, even if it's correct according to the description of the movement.

Prone Position

Roll over on your stomach and lie firmly on the floor. Are you lying straight in relation to your length axis?

Place a couple of pillows under your ankles and give yourself time to relax all the parts of your body; how does it feel?

Bend one leg, grasp your ankle, and slowly pull it toward your buttock on the same side. Your partner can do this for you, but be careful not to use force and to watch out that the lower part of the leg isn't bent out of axis so that it points toward the center or out to the side.

Do you feel the stretch on the front of your thigh and in your groin and stomach? Let go of the stretch so that your leg drops down again and try this with your other leg.

How is your leg lying now? Try to tense your buttocks. What happens with your legs and feet?

If you stand or sit with tense buttocks, the position of your legs will also be affected. Can you let go around your hip joints so that your legs and heels roll out a little?

If not, then try to turn them in a little from your hip joint so that both your knees and big toes point toward each other a bit. How does it feel?

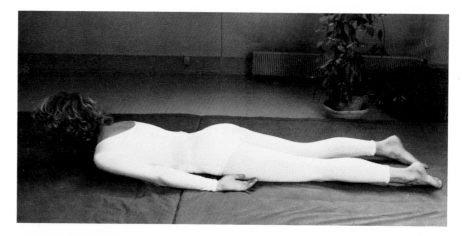

Sea Lion

Place your arms along your sides and your forehead against the floor. See whether you can get in touch with the uppermost vertebra in your neck and begin to bend you head backward from there, but be careful not to bend so much that there isn't any mobility left in your neck's lowest vertebra.

Let your chin slide off the floor, and see whether you can make an even curve with your neck. Breathe deeply with the top of your chest and try to include your back's topmost vertebra in the movement.

It's tough. In our daily life we most often use these joints to bend forward, so it's not strange if it takes a little time before your muscles and joints do what you want.

Let your chest expand outward. Can you also make it expand to the sides by bringing your shoulder blades down your back?

Don't go too far up. It's better to stay in a position where you can feel in touch with the movement without becoming tense or letting the curve in the

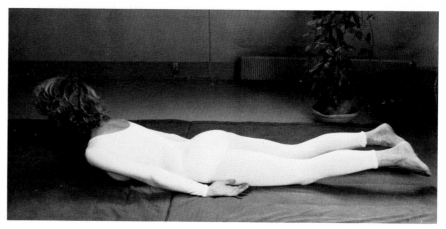

small of your back take over the entire movement. Stop if you feel any discomfort in your back.

Take a deep breath once more and slide down again to a lying position. How did your neck and back muscles work? Did you get in touch with the stretch in the front of your body?

Sea Lion with Hands on Floor

Place the upper part of your arms away from your body with your forearms bent and your hands palms down on the floor, level with your ears. If your shoulders are pulled up, you can bring your arms down a little and out to the side.

Can you get good contact with your hands?

Try now to do the same movement as before, but this time don't bring your head back so much. Curve your neck slightly, and try to include the uppermost joint in your back in the movement.

Stop and breathe deeply and then slowly continue joint by joint. Now, since you have the support of your

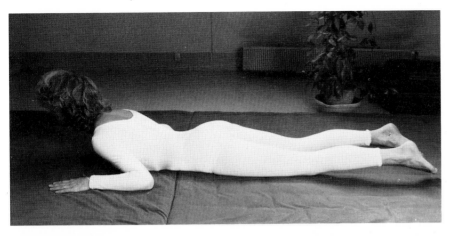

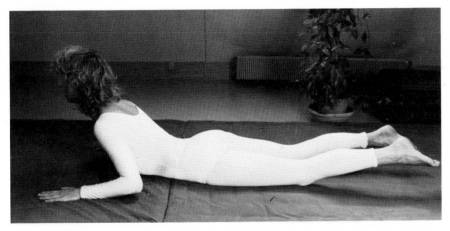

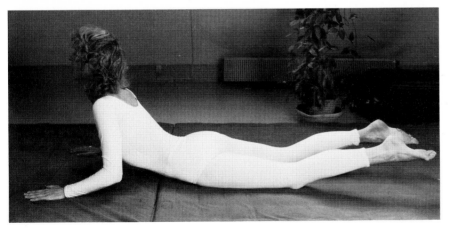

hands and forearms, you can try to come up a little farther, but don't push with your arms. It's your body that should do the movement.

Try to draw your shoulder blades down your back so that they slide into the curve of your back, and let the movement expand so that you push your groin down against the floor. Stop if you feel any discomfort in your back.

What happens to your legs? If they want to pop up, then let them. They do this because of the connection between your back and the muscles of your seat and legs. Watch an infant who's lying on its stomach lift its head; its entire body is included in the movement.

Let your arms slide forward as you let go of the stretch while exhaling and fall down, though not so fast that you hurt your nose.

Did you feel the difference between these two movements?

The Cat Stretch

Imagine that a rope is tied around your groin and behind. In order to bring you up from the prone position, I place myself behind you by your feet and pull the rope.

You can make the rope real by having your partner place a hand on each of your hip joints (no higher up than where your thighs meet your hips) and pull you up backward and at a slant.

Push off with your hands as you bend your knees and hips, so that your behind points toward your friend. Stop for a moment and feel the stretch spread from your arms to your behind, and then let the weight of your body take over the work, pulling you back to lie with your stomach against your thighs and your arms stretched out by your head.

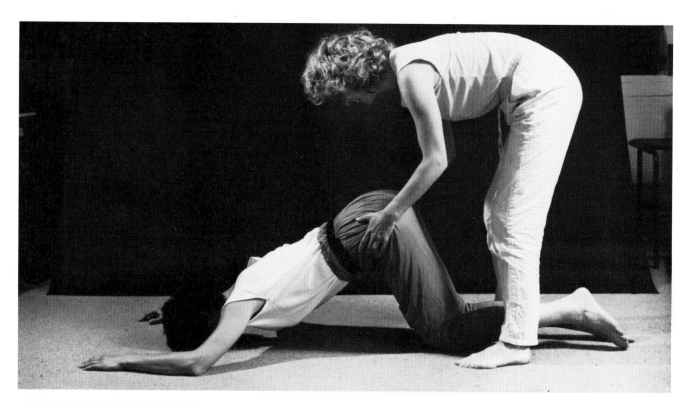

Rest a few minutes, and then roll up vertebra by vertebra, pelvis first. It is easier to use the weight of your behind to come up from here if your partner's hands are placed on your buttocks, lightly pressing down toward the floor, thus emphasizing the movement.

Now that you're familiar with the movements and positions discussed so far, is there a change in how you relate to your body and how you use it?

What about your daily life? Do you feel any change?

Try to concentrate from time to time during the day on how you move. If necessary, go back to the beginning sections and read them again. This will help you get the greatest possible benefit out of this book.

Sitting Movements (Floor)

Shake your legs and sit comfortably on your seat bones.

Seated Hamstring Stretches

Stretch your legs straight out from your torso. If it makes you round your back or if it feels uncomfortably tight in the hollows of your knees, put pillows under your behind and your knees until you can sit up without tensing.

Then stretch the back of each leg, one at a time, by bringing your heel forward along the floor with your foot flexed and your toes pointing straight up in the air.

Where do you feel the stretch?

Afterward, you can try stretching out one leg and then the other several times in a gentle rhythm.

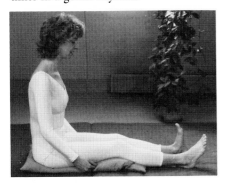

Let go of the stretch and shake your legs.

If it's difficult for you to sit with your legs straight in front of you, especially if it feels uncomfortable in your back, then save the next movement until you feel more comfortable in this position.

Hanging Forward

If you can sit this way without discomfort, then try to fall forward from your hip joint and let yourself hang with your body's weight. Breathe deeply and

feel how the stretch spreads.

It's important that you don't force yourself down. Your back is vulnerable in this position.

If you feel like doing a larger stretch, hang with your torso and stretch out one heel at a time as you did before.

Let go of the stretch and slowly pull yourself up from your hips and then go through your back. Can you let your head hang heavily until it comes up as the final part of the movement?

If you find that some of your muscles are tense in these movements—for instance, if your knees stick up a lot or if you can't move from your hips—then hang there awhile and let gravity pull you.

You should do this stretch before you plunge into modern dance, where

the stretches are greater because the rhythm of the movements is faster.

The Cradle

Pull your legs up in front of your body with your feet flat on the floor and grasp your legs just below your knees. Feel whether you have good contact with the palms of your hands, and then release your hips and the small of your back so that you slowly roll your sacrum down toward the floor at the same time that you stretch out your arms.

Let your head hang forward heavily, and try to see whether you can place the vertebrae of your back one by one on the floor until you come to the point where you are shaped like a cradle. Can

you find the balancing point where your legs and torso are like equal weights?

Before you get so far down that your torso becomes heaviest, pull yourself up again by stretching out your legs and straightening your body all the way

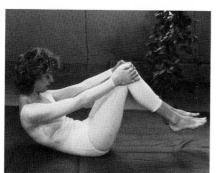

your shoulders and between your shoulder blades?

Try to retain the feeling of gravity in your body and roll all the way down through your back, vertebra by vertebra, until you're lying on the floor. Then release your legs, let your feet drop down and slide your legs down to the floor.

How was it? Were you able to feel your balance and the different stretches in your body?

If you feel like it, stretch before you sit up again.

Squatting

Sit down on a pillow with your legs bent up in front of your body; are you sitting on your seat bones and are your feet placed firmly on the floor?

Lean forward against your thighs and let your head hang forward. If this

doesn't bring you up to a squatting position, then push yourself up the last part of the way with your hands.

Find out how much of the soles of your feet you can keep on the floor without losing your balance.

If it's difficult to keep your balance, you can move your legs out to the sides a little so that your torso is between your legs. Does this help? You can also try a larger pillow under your behind.

Now try using only your legs to get up. Push off with your feet and push your behind backward as you slowly straighten your legs and roll up through the joints in your back. Use what you tried when you rolled up in a standing position and let your head and arms hang heavily.

If there are two of you, your partner should be in front of you and should give you time to stand rather than yank

down from your hip joints.

If it felt good, try it again. Think this time about your elbows and try to draw your shoulder blades down your back. Can you hang by your arms and shoulders without using any strength in them so that your muscles are stretched from your arms all the way around to

Could you maintain the stretch around your shoulders on the way up?

If the movement feels good to you, you can also try (with or without a partner) to get up with your neck and head lifted, as in the picture.

Start by imagining that someone is pulling you up by your hair, and push off with your feet as before.

Finish off by stretching yourself slowly and steadily, one side at a time.

you up by the arms. Most of the movement should be yours.

Bend down by the knees and hips as if you both were accordions, and find the right distance between you that allows you to hang from your partner without getting a rounded back.

Can you both find the point where you can give each other a stretch from your arms and around your shoulders to the spot between the shoulder blades?

Play a little with the weight of your body. Both of you should be constantly aware of what is happening with your shoulders and elbows.

Then push off with your legs as you did before, and roll up to a standing position, vertebra by vertebra, your partner's weight providing a counterbalance that supports you.

Standing Movements

Start by using some of the movements described in the previous sections to find the spot where you stand with the least possible tension and where your feet are planted firmly on the floor.

Shift Weight and Balance

Imagine that your body is being lifted up so that your back and the back of your neck become longer. Feel the weight on your feet. Can you shift your weight over to one foot without moving your body all that much?

Place your hands on your hip joints and try again to shift your weight. Feel whether you stay within your length axis, and avoid bending your hip to the side.

This should result in a very small shift of your entire body all the way down to your feet, so small that it almost can't be seen.

Can you bend your free leg a little?

If the movement was difficult to do without moving your body away from your length axis, position yourself with one foot on a telephone book or a similar firm elevation.

This position will also make it easier to do things with your free leg. Can you find your balance with all of your weight on the one leg?

With your hand, grasp the back of the thigh of your free leg and push it. Can you let your hip joint go so that your leg hangs loose?

Bring your arms out to the sides; this helps your balance. Swing your leg back and forth, and then bend your leg

up toward your stomach and out to your side. Can you also stretch it forward, then bring it out to your side and back?

Shift legs, find your balance, and try again.

Shift legs once more, and this time try to come forward from your hip joint. Stretch your arm forward and stretch your free leg backward.

Shift legs and try again. Play with the different ways you can move your leg; you'll have use for these positions in modern dance.

The next movement is a combination of several of the previous ones, and a standing variation of the movement in which you stretched out your arm as you came forward with your body from your hip joint (page 41).

Stretch Forward and Pull Back

Step down from the elevation and position yourself well, with your toes pointing straight ahead and with just less than the width of your hips between your feet. Take a step forward with your right foot and bend your knee and hip so that you lean forward over your front leg as your back leg is stretched out without your heel being lifted from the floor.

Can you sense a straight line from your left heel up through your leg to your left hip and your back and on to your head?

Stand awhile and feel how your weight is divided between your front and back foot.

Do you get a stretch in your back leg?

Push with your front leg so that you come up again with your body and move your weight back on your left leg without moving your feet.

Shift legs and try again. Shift your weight forward and move it back again.

Can you feel how the movement of your entire body can come from your feet?

Shift legs and come forward again; bring your right arm forward this time. If you are standing properly, your right leg and arm should now be forward.

Straight in front of your chest is a

very beautiful flower.

Come forward from your hip joint and reach for it. Use what you worked with in the arm stretch on page 41.

Do you feel the connection in your body?

Pick the flower and push yourself back again with your weight on your back leg. Try it a couple of times, and shift legs occasionally.

Now there's a new flower even farther away. In order to reach it, you have to bend your knee and hip even more and stretch your arm out slowly and steadily. Be careful not to lose your balance.

Can you keep your heels on the floor? How are your back and arms connected?

Pick the flower and push yourself back while you straighten your hip joint. Pull your leg back and shake your feet.

Try the same thing with your other leg forward.

Vary the movement as you like. Try the movement when sitting at a large table, or over a coffee table. Make the stretches short so that you can push yourself forward and pull yourself back quickly, or do them slowly and steadily.

Play with your body's opportunities for movement.

Roll Down from a Standing Position

In the Basic Standing Position (page 23), you rolled down from your neck's uppermost vertebra until you were looking at your stomach.

If it felt good last time, you can now roll farther down.

Start by pulling yourself up a little so that your back and neck lengthen, and then roll slowly downward. Pay attention to your balance.

Bend as much in your knees and hips as you need to in order to maintain

your balance, and let your behind stick out more and more.

If there are parts that don't want to go along, then stop for a moment and breathe deeply. Roll down until your behind points up. Stop if you become tense in order to maintain your balance.

Stay there and feel the stretch.

Are your arms, shoulders, and head completely heavy, and is your weight evenly divided between both your feet?

Come forward a little so that your weight rests a little more on the balls of your feet than on your heels.

Can you straighten out your knees? If they hurt too much, then bend them again.

Now push off from your feet as you lower your knees and roll your behind underneath you.

Do you feel that your pelvis is pulling up the small of your back?

Come up joint by joint while your legs straighten out at a tempo that suits you, and roll on through your neck's

58

seven small vertebrae with your head like a heavy ball that comes up at the last moment. Did it feel different this time?

Standing Stretch

This time, bring your slightly bent arms forward and up alongside your head. Can you let your shoulder blades slide down along your back and avoid arching the small of your back? Breathe deeply and stretch yourself up, little by little, one arm at a time. Try to stretch from the small of your back to your fingertips, slowly and steadily, and feel the weight in your body as much as possible.

If there are two of you, your partner's hands can be placed on the small of your back and follow your stretching movement up, being careful not to push the shoulder blade up. When your friend lets go of the stretch as you reach your hands, let your arms fall down along your sides.

Sitting Movements (Chair)

Sit down on a chair that suits you. If the chair has a back, move forward on the seat so there's room to round your back. Lift your legs one at a time and feel their weight; does your foot hang down?

Let your arms hang heavily and see whether you can pull your shoulder blades down your back a little without pushing with your arms. A good way to get in touch with them is to pull them up and back a little. Then bring them down to relax.

Feel the Weight in Each Other's Legs

This section and the next one are addressed to your partner.

Position yourself in front of your friend's right leg and hold it with both hands around the thigh. Check to see whether you have a good grip, and lift the leg up slowly until the toes rise just above the floor.

Be sure to bend at the knees and hips while lifting so that you don't strain your back by rounding it.

Hold the leg; is your partner letting you support the whole weight of it? Does the foot hang loosely from the ankle joint?

Bring the leg down with the foot on the floor again.

In order to feel whether the hip joint is relaxed, place a flat hand on the thigh and try to push it slightly toward the center and back out to the side. Does the leg want to go along?

Ask how the leg and foot are posi-

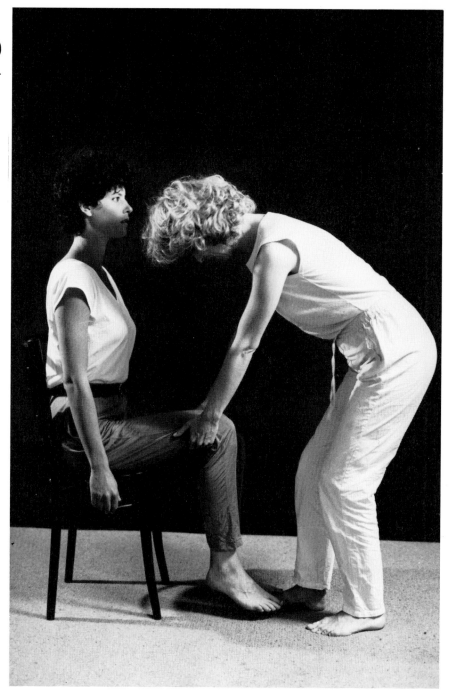

tioned. Try to figure out what feels right together.

Move so that you're standing just in front of the left leg and try again.

Feel the Weight of Each Other's Arms

Now place yourself so that you are facing the sitting person's right side and hold the upper arm with both hands.

Lift the arm slowly out to the side while taking care not to lift the shoulder. Both of you should look for a feeling of weight in the arm; it can be seen by the forearm and hand hanging loosely down.

If the arm is resisting, try to lift it a little bit farther out and give yourself a little time before you bring the arm back again.

Ask if there is a difference between the arms before you try the other arm. It's important that you gently hold the arm and leg a bit before you begin to lift and that you do it slowly; otherwise, reflexes will make the muscles tense up.

Chair Arch

Do you remember Sea Lion (page 50), where you were supposed to include the upper part of your back in a backward arch?

Much of the same movement can be done in your chair.

Start by making a small arch backward in your neck's upper and middle vertebrae, and concentrate on involving the vertebrae at the base of the neck and in the top part of the back in the movement. Let the movement continue down your back to your hip joint and stick your behind out. Be careful if you

have back problems, and stop if you feel any pain.

How was it?

You can also try to start the arch down from your hip joint as you did in Basic Sitting Position (page 21), but be careful not to arch the small of your back too much, or you may limit the mobility of your back's uppermost joint.

When you arch in other positions (for instance, sitting on your heels), you can try to get more movement in the joints in the same way.

Now round your back by moving backward from your hip joint and slowly let go, joint by joint, up through your back and neck. Stay here awhile and roll up again.

Have you found the position where you feel that all parts of your body are resting on top of each other?

The Shoulder Elevator

Draw up your shoulders using those muscles that run from the back of your neck out along your shoulders. You may have to work a little at getting the right muscles to lift your shoulders.

It may help to have your partner's hands placed on your shoulder muscles.

Can you relax the rest of your body so that you don't pull your head down or push up with your arms?

Slowly let go of the tension, then try to let go even more, so that your shoulders come down farther than they were before you drew them up.

Lowering Your Shoulders

By using the muscles you have between your shoulder blades, rhomboideus and trapezius, you can draw your shoulder blades down and in toward each other.

If you're working with a partner, hands placed on these muscles can help you feel where they are.

Can you let your arms be passive and avoid tensing in the small of your back? If your head wants to travel backward a little with the movement, that's fine.

Let go of everything all at once and let your head, shoulders, and the upper part of your back come forward to hang. Stay here a few moments and breathe deeply. Where do you feel the stretch?

Then pull yourself up by starting from the bottommost part of your back, which you have rounded, and slowly roll up through your back and your seven neck vertebrae, ending with your head.

Again, a hand following the movement is a help.

Now, how do your shoulders feel? Are they positioned differently than be-

Neck and Head Rotation

Drop your head straight over to one side with your ear down toward your shoulder. Let it hang awhile by its own gravity; it should feel rather heavy.

Draw it up again slowly by using the muscles of the other side.

Did you feel a connection between your head and shoulder? Where did you feel the stretch?

Drop your head to the other side and let it hang. Does it stretch the same muscles as the other side?

Draw your head up again and let it slide down toward the first shoulder; stay here awhile and then roll slowly forward, so that your entire face turns in toward your chest.

Don't forget to breathe, and stop when you feel like staying with a stretch.

Do the movement so slowly that the weight of your head passively stretches out the muscles of your neck and

shoulders. Roll all the way over to your other shoulder.

Draw your head up when you have had enough of stretching, or if you feel that the front of your neck is being stretched too much.

If not, continue the movement backward while you try to get it to spread down to your back's uppermost joint. Be careful not to stay in this position too long; it may be strenuous for your neck muscles.

Roll on to your other shoulder and draw your head up. Wait a little before you drop your head down to the other shoulder, repeating the movement in the opposite direction.

Hanging Forward

Try again to pull yourself up a little. Can you, despite the fact that you are sitting down, get a feeling of being raised?

With your long, straight back, fall

fore? The familiarity you gain through using your muscles like this may help you to notice when they tense up in other situations.

But don't force your shoulders down if you have good reasons for drawing them up. Then you'll just shift the tension to another spot.

Move yourself back on the seat a little if your back is tired, and let the back of the chair support your back.

forward from your hip joints and place your stomach against your thighs. Then release your head,¹ shoulders, and arms. Feel your forehead, eyes, jaw, and tongue. Try to relax your entire face.

Breathe deeply. How far out into your pelvis and your behind can you feel that you're expanding?

Try to let go as if you were going to break wind. If you really have to, don't hold back.

How does it feel to stay this way? If you have a feeling of falling forward, you can move your behind a little farther back on the chair, and if necessary place a pillow under your feet. Does it help?

A pair of hands placed firmly at the very bottom of your back also help you to feel more of a sense of gravity there.

Come up again by drawing your pelvis up and back a little so that it drags your body along. Try to maintain a feeling of weightiness as you lift your pelvis up from your hip joints and roll up through your back, vertebra by ver-

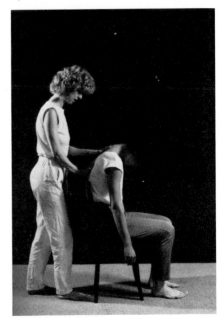

tebra. Let your head hang heavily all the way up so that it comes up last.

If you are working with a partner, try to describe to each other what you feel as you move.

Getting Up

Now try to stand without using any strength in your torso.

Place one foot just underneath the chair, tilt forward at your hips, and push with your feet so that you use the muscles in your legs to get up.

By using your legs and hip joints, you protect your back from being strained. It may take a while to get the hang of it, but with practice you will, and then you'll be able to use this technique in a lot of situations, especially in modern dance.

Finish off by stretching.

If you have a stiff neck or your back is sore, do these movements very carefully until you find those that feel the best. It's extremely important that you don't push yourself or work too quickly, and that you don't roll your head back if your neck hurts. Otherwise you risk making it worse.

It is the passive stretches, where relaxed muscles let themselves give and be stretched, that can help the most.

Trust what you feel, what you need, and what feels good for you; but if you have the slightest feeling that something may be wrong, never postpone a visit to the doctor.

Foot Movements

The Foot's Mobility

Sit on the floor, or on a bed or couch which is firm enough not to rock beneath you.

Find a comfortable position where you can hold one foot in your hands without tensing your body, and feel the foot resting in your hands.

Place your fingertips on the sole of your foot with your thumbs on top, and try to see whether you can fold the foot down around your fingers.

Does your foot give?

Check your entire foot. The many small joints are well served by being moved.

Now try this with your other foot.

Rotation of Toes

Grasp the bottom part of your big toe just above the joint to the foot with your thumb and index finger and see if you can rotate the joint. Turn it one way and then the other, but be careful

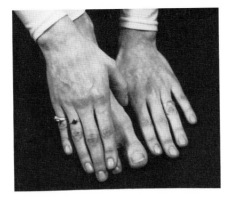

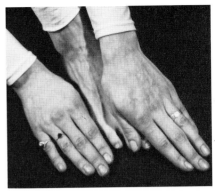

not to push it. Your toes may not be used to these movements.

Then give your toe a little stretch out in the direction of the foot's axis and release it. Could you feel the stretch?

Stretch all your toes this way and feel whether your feet feel different afterward. Did the foot you worked with become warmer?

Now try your other foot.

Now put both feet down; are they positioned well? Spread all your toes, curl them underneath your foot, and relax them.

Push with Your Toes

Place your hand along the inside edge of your foot and see whether you can push it by moving your big toe outward to the side. It may be difficult. Socks and shoes often squeeze our toes in the opposite direction.

In order to keep the other toes still, you can place your other hand on top of them and try again.

You can help your toe along by lightly pressing on the side of the arch of the foot. The muscle that controls the movement runs here.

You may not be able to do this

movement with your big toe the first few times you try. That shouldn't make you give up. All of a sudden it will begin to move, but don't keep at it for too long a time. If the muscles aren't used to these movements, they can become cramped.

Exercising these muscles can bring your big toes farther out to the side, which among other things means a lot for their ability to push off when walking.

Strengthening the muscles in the arch of the foot can also prevent the arch from dropping, which causes you to turn in at your ankle joints.

Try the same thing with your little toe by placing one hand along the outer edge of your foot and the other hand on top of the rest of your toes. Can you get your little toe to move outward?

Try with your other foot.

Your little toes may be even more resistant than your big toes. Be patient. They'll come around after a while.

Shake your feet. How do they feel?

When you know the foot movements, you can work with them while you are doing something else, for instance, watching television or talking with friends.

Walking

The Senses of Your Feet

Take a little walk barefoot, on a carpet. How does it feel? Walk on a bare floor; if there are cracks and crumbs, see whether you can feel them.

Cold and warm, crooked and straight, rough and smooth—can you feel the difference? Expose your feet to as many sensations as possible; you can feel a great deal with them.

The Foot's Mobility in Walking

Take a step forward heel first, letting your weight slowly shift over to the foot in front at the same time that the foot in back gradually leaves the floor.

Use what you learned from the standing movements about shifting your weight.

Take one more step and this time see if your toes can point straight ahead.

Slowly shift your weight to your front foot, which little by little rolls down to the floor as the big toe on your back foot pushes off and is the last part to leave the floor when you swing your leg forward to a new step.

Balloon Walking

Without tensing up, can you pull yourself up a little and feel light, as if you had a balloon in your body? Come forward and up when you walk so that you don't drop your weight heavily with each step.

Try to walk on your toes, and then down on your entire foot again.

Let your arms swing with the movement. Imagine you're a person on the moon who needs only to push off slightly to fly on to the next step.

What happens to the other parts of your body if you keep your arms stiff? How does it feel if your body's tilt and weight go backward?

Bring your weight forward again and let your arms swing with the walking movement; can you feel the difference?

Try to tighten your buttocks while you walk, and then let go of them again. What happened?

Walk this way, with a feeling of lightness and with your big toe pushing you off, in other situations. It can feel completely liberating.

In working with modern dance you will constantly come across movements where you have to feel lifted up, a feeling that can actually make you about an inch taller. If you find this difficult, then go back to the movements in this section and to the standing movements in the second section until you understand the feeling.

Use this book to look up things in any order you like. As mentioned earlier, afspaending movements don't end where modern dance movements begin. There is no fixed boundary between the two, and you can put together your own combination of afspaending and modern dance based on what you like to work with most.

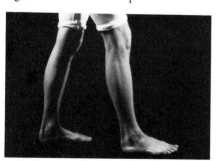
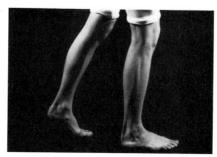
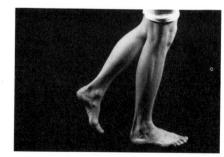

Isadora Duncan dances. Pastel sketches by Maurice Denis, about 1910.

MODERN DANCE

As a dancer, I turned toward afspaending in order to answer some of the personal questions that had arisen after several years of dance training. Afspaending answered most of these questions in a physical rather than intellectual way, and the questions themselves are impossible to describe in words. Yet one important thing that afspaending gave me was *time*—time to listen to my body, to hear it, and subsequently to work with it. All this took place during my first stay in Denmark (1976–78), when I studied afspaending with one of its founders, Marussia Berg. I returned to Denmark in 1981 and started teaching, and I turned to afspaending again, although in a different way than before. As modern dance is quite new to the Danes, I found that some of my students were late starters, and the energy blocks in their bodies, which had accumulated after years without training, were preventing them from making any progress without straining themselves. It was at this point that Margit and I started teaching together.

Compared to an afspaending session, a dance class is a fast, demanding, and rhythmic experience. It concerns itself with the breath of life flowing outward and into space, and considers such things as form, structure, composition of phrases—working with repetition toward the goal of perfection. It is technique; a spiritual craft that uses the body as an instrument of expression. The dancer is given an opportunity to explore, with guidance, the world of movement, which is limitless. There is always the drive to better oneself, to go a little farther, to feel a little deeper. This is an exciting process, sometimes frustrating yet always interesting.

I have not attempted to imitate these dance classes in the following chapters. I realize that the energy and direct contact between teacher and student is impossible to re-create. What the following chapters offer is time to explore and discover the basic elements found in dance, using as a foundation the different movements covered in the previous section.

The warm-up that follows, which I designed, is a result of my varied dance studies, and has been transformed over the years by different discoveries made while working alone and while teaching others. It has also been influenced by the awareness of tension that is the central aspect of afspaending, and the reader will notice direct connections between the previous chapters and the following ones.

Because this book has been designed for use in a limited amount of space, I have eliminated large "traveling" phrases, or sequences of movements that take you over a large expanse of floor, and have concentrated on the lying, sitting, and standing aspects of the warm-ups. Jumps have also been left out, because I feel a photograph and words cannot relate the groundwork and understanding that a simple jump contains. It is something that takes the guidance of a teacher.

The reader should take advantage of the individual exploration one can accomplish by working alone. The goal is not to skim through the movements or imitate the pictures, but rather to find personal understanding of and expression in the kinetics and aesthetics of dance.

WARM-UP 1

When you start working with the first part of the warm-up, I suggest you work at a slow and flowing pace. That way you'll have time to feel each movement.
Later, the movements will change; they'll either be more forceful or faster, which will require you to have more control over your body. Until you reach this control, you'll gain most by working slowly.

Movement Combinations: Lying Down

To have contact with the floor is a basic element of modern dance that separates it from other forms of dance.

Going down to the floor is a difficult movement to do without letting the weight drop down and losing control over the body. It demands that tension be maintained while moving toward the floor.

Find the Floor

In this first warm-up combination, you'll lower your body toward the floor by using the force of gravity. Place your legs slightly apart, with your arms relaxed by your sides and your weight evenly distributed over both legs. Place one hand behind your head and guide your head down toward the floor so that your torso forms a curve. Bend your knees when your head approaches your legs.

While you are on your way down, feel that your spine and back muscles are really being stretched.

Lower your bottom and continue to travel down toward the floor. Try to feel relaxed in your body while you're moving, and just before your bottom touches the floor, place both hands in front of you and let them quickly slide backward so that they catch your weight as your body slides out and down on the floor.

It's necessary to have a certain amount of tension in your pelvic area if your body is not to *fall down* to the floor. The control of your body begins at this point, a control that will help to direct energy instead of blocking it.

Roll slowly down to the floor while you stretch your legs out and slip your torso down.

When you're lying on the floor, really stretch your whole body and then relax.

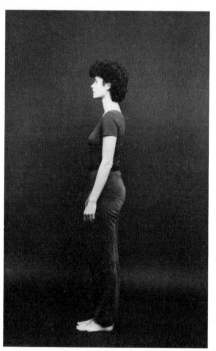

Divide Your Body

While you are lying on the floor, feel the various points of your body.

HEAD

TORSO

ARM with ARM

CENTER

LEGS

FEET

This is a very simplified diagram of the parts of the body and how they relate.

If you move each part of the body separately (arms, legs, etc.), you will begin to notice that each movement begins from an inner activity of the nerves, rather than an outer activity of the muscles. You will also notice how one part of the body influences the other parts when moving. For example, when you lift your arm above your head, the back moves. Try to experiment by moving the different parts of the body.

We will now start by working the lower part of the body and seeing how each part influences the other.

Turn-Out

Lie on your back so that you are comfortable. Stretch your legs straight down from your torso and make sure that they are parallel, the back of your legs resting against the floor and your knees pointing straight up to the ceiling. Continue the straight line you are creating with your legs by sending the energy into your feet.

Place your hands on your groin muscles and let your right leg slowly fall outward. You should be able to feel how the rotation in your hip socket stretches your groin muscles, and how your foot automatically follows the leg outward. This position is called "turn-out." It describes the rotation that begins in the hip socket, *not* in the knee, ankle, or foot.

Shake your legs out to release the tension, and repeat the combination with your left leg.

Alternate 4 times between a parallel position and a turned-out position with each leg.

Pointing the Foot

In order to create a straight line for your body's energy, it's necessary that you stretch yourself all the way out so that the energy can follow the lines of your body.

One way to do this is to extend or lengthen the various parts of your body out into the surrounding space.

When you stretch your foot, you'll work with two places in your foot: your heel and your arch. Both will influence other parts of the body.

Keep your feet in a parallel position. Stretch your right foot by slowly drawing your heel up toward the back of your leg and pointing your toes downward. This way the foot arches naturally and the muscles in your leg follow. Focus the energy through your leg into your foot and out into space.

Let go of the movement by returning to a relaxed parallel position.

Alternately move your foot from a relaxed parallel position to a pointed parallel position. Repeat the combination 4 times. Shake your right leg out and repeat the movement with your left foot.

Place your legs in a turned-out position and repeat the movement. Remember that the turn-out starts in the hip socket.

Feel how pointing the foot influences all the muscles in the leg.

Flexing the Foot

It's characteristic of warm-up movements in modern dance that opposing movements follow one after the other.

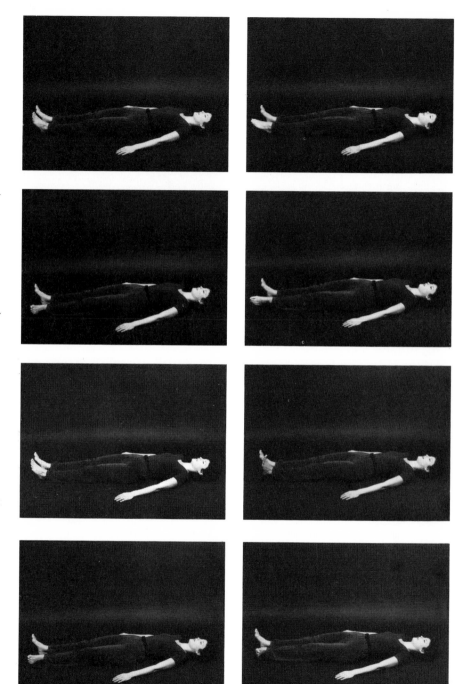

For example, after you point the foot, you should do the opposite—that is, flex it.

This use of opposing movements gives the body a more thorough self-awareness and a greater expressiveness of motion.

Flexing the foot is the opposite of pointing it; the back part is lengthened, extending the energy out into space.

Pointing the foot extends the line of the leg down through the foot and toes, while flexing bends the ankle, bringing the foot upward, making a line perpendicular to the leg.

When pointing, you extend the front leg muscles (those facing the ceiling). When flexing, you extend the back leg muscles (those facing the floor).

Place your feet in a parallel position. Stretch out your right heel away from your leg into space. Notice how the foot forms a right angle in relation to the leg.

Alternate between flexing and reflexing the leg and foot 4 times. Relax and shake out your leg. Repeat the combination with your left foot.

Then execute the combination in a turned-out position, first with your right leg and then with your left.

Combining Movements

We now have four positions to work with that involve our feet and legs. When combining these four positions, concentrate on your heel as the navigator of your foot's movements, and remember that turned-out positions start from the hip sockets.

Start with your right leg and move through the four positions: *point parallel, flexed parallel, point turn-out,* and *flexed turn-out.*

It's important that you try to get your foot to *slide* from one position to the next. Try to avoid jerking, and make sure you move at a slow pace.

Repeat the combination 4 times, shake out your leg, and repeat the movement with your left foot.

Grow Through Your Legs

One of the goals in this warm-up is to learn to lift your weight up and out of your body. This kind of movement expresses a quality of lightness.

All too often in daily life, our weight is allowed to drop into our lower trunk, making it more difficult to remain light on our feet and throwing off the balance in the entire body.

The goal is to keep the movement's energy flowing outward, avoiding blocks by finding new channels of release for it—upward, downward, out to the sides, etc.

Now, when you are lying on the floor, try to concentrate on letting your energy flow down your legs and out through the tips of your toes. If you can find this feeling in a prone position, it'll be easier to execute the energy release in the standing combinations without your weight dropping down, making it difficult to move freely.

This combination concentrates on flexing and relaxing your leg, using a slide motion with a constant, flowing energy.

At this point, I'd like to introduce two new terms. While executing the phrases in the warm-up, some parts of the body are more directly involved than others. This doesn't mean that the whole body isn't working; but for simplicity's sake we refer to the active leg as the *working leg*, and the stationary leg as the *standing leg*.

Start by placing your left foot on the floor so that your leg forms a 45 degree angle. This is the standing leg. You will not work directly with it, but be aware of it.

Slowly stretch your right leg and point the foot so that the energy is sent out through your toes. Then, slowly lift your right leg up to your chest by bending at the knee and folding in at the groin area.

When you flex your leg, your spine is well stretched out; in the parlance of modern dance, it extends out into space.

Hold this position, but keep breathing into your body. Notice how the energy seems to flow out of the spine into space. Two types of movements are occurring here: a stretch out into space (the spine), and a contraction inward with the leg.

It's important to work slowly, not jerking your muscles into place, but letting them gently slide from one position to the next.

Leave the position by letting your right foot touch the floor and then slowly sliding it along the floor until your leg is completely extended and the foot is pointed. Finish off the combination by bringing your right foot to a flexed position.

Repeat the combination 4 times, shake out your right leg, and then bring your right foot in to the same position as the left foot while the bottom of your spine stretches out. Repeat the combination with your left leg, now the working leg.

The "Center"—Your Body's Energy Point

Isadora Duncan, one of the innovators of modern dance, used to stand in front of a mirror and observe her body while she looked for the starting point of every single movement.

She said that during this meditation it became more and more apparent that for her the solar plexus was the spot in the body where each movement began.

Martha Graham, who created a technique based on "contraction" and "release," located the "center" further down, in the pelvic region.

Even though the exact location of this spot is open to discussion, teachers of modern dance are in general agreement that such an area actually exists.

I won't point out a particular spot in the pelvic area for you to concentrate on, because I believe that we all have our own individual energy point, but I do believe that it's located in the lower part of the torso, simply because this is where life begins.

When we get more into the combinations of movements, the term *center* will come into play more often. It is important to understand this term's relation to the movements, so that the tension that accompanies movement can be focused on the correct areas.

Start by repeating the movements that we've gone through so far, this time thinking about your center as the spot where they originate. Even though you haven't directly "moved" this part of the body through space, it doesn't mean that energy hasn't been moving internally.

77

Opening Out

Now repeat the previous movements, but in a turned-out position. Think of the center while executing the movements.

Can you feel the energy?

Extend your standing leg and keep it extended during the entire combination.

Begin by stretching out both legs in a turned-out position.

Then draw your right leg up toward you as you lengthen the lowest part of your back. Keep your hips on the floor. As you draw the right leg up toward your torso, imagine that a string is attached to the middle of your knee and is pulling your leg through space.

Now extend your leg up and then slowly let it return to the floor.

Shake your legs out and change legs so that your right leg becomes the

standing leg while your left leg works.
Repeat the combination 4 times.

Connecting Parallel and Turned-Out Positions Through Space

The next combination is to be done very slowly so that you have time to feel how the energy of movement, and thereby the "tension point," is located in your center. Try to keep the rest of

the body fairly relaxed, with the center acting as a furnace for the kinetic energy.

It's possible that your body isn't ready yet for this movement.

If this is the case, then return to the afspaending movement called Lying Flower (page 46) and the warm-up combinations above, and repeat these until you feel ready to continue.

Start with both legs in a parallel position.

With the help of your center, slowly lift your legs up while you flex at the knees and at the crease that separates your leg from your torso. Can you feel the stretch in your spine?

Try to keep your shoulders and hips on the floor, and let your neck remain relaxed. If you feel that you are tensing, then shake your body loose and start from the beginning. Slowly open your legs out into space, but don't let

them fall out, causing the back to arch. Stay in this position, feeling your lower back open up. Try to relax the body by controlling the movement from your center.

Bring your feet down to the floor and let them slide along the floor while your legs stretch out.

Shake your legs and repeat 4 times.

Borrowing from the Past

The various parts of the body and their mutual relationships change when the body is moving. These changes create shapes in space, and these shapes are a large part of the aesthetics of modern dance.

For instance, Isadora Duncan studied ancient Greek vases in order to find inspiration for her choreography.

The positions and movements that Ruth St. Denis (another pioneer in modern dance) created came largely from Indian and oriental positions.

While you execute the following combinations, you should try to become aware of the shapes and figures that the contour of your body creates. At the same time try to feel these shapes *inside* your body by working with the inner dynamics that lie behind every single movement.

You can also begin to recognize how certain movements express certain emotions. For example, suddenly moving inward expresses a bound quality, while slowly moving outward expresses a flowing quality.

Moving Your Legs and Feet Through Space

It's important that the movement energy that lies behind this combination be steady and slow. You shouldn't divide the movements into two parts, extending and flexing; instead, connect them by using the image of climbing up a hill (extending), and immediately climbing down again (flexing).

Lie in a parallel position with your left leg on the floor (the standing leg).

Draw your right leg up toward your torso as you flex at the ankle, knee, and hip. In one steady movement stretch your right leg and point your right foot, barely off the floor.

Repeat the flexing and extending movements 2 more times by bringing your leg higher and higher into space with each stretch.

Now reverse the combination as you

79

let your right leg stretch outward, getting closer to the floor with each extension. End by having both legs extended.

Shake both legs and repeat the combination with your left leg as the working leg. Concentrate on the hip of the standing leg so that it doesn't roll up or in while the working leg is in action.

From here move in reverse to the starting position. You can also go forward and backward through many of the following combinations.

Fetal Position

In this sequence, your body is fully stretched as you pull away from your center with your upper body and let your lower body travel out into space.

Roll over on your right side and really stretch out as you send your body's energy out through your fingers and toes. It's important that you stretch from your back, in the same way that you have stretched in the afspaending movements, so that your shoulders don't rise up and the small of your back doesn't arch.

Now slowly pull yourself in, contracting the body, as you imagine that there is something lightly pressing against the pelvic area and making you curl inward. Continue this movement until your head touches your knees.

Feel the stretch in your spine.

Now, do the movement in reverse by working yourself out into space. Begin this movement by arching the back and at the same time moving your arms and legs away from your center. As in the earlier combinations, you are working with the feeling of stretching, but here you are stretching your entire body out into space. When you fold your body inward, you contract your entire body by pressing back at the center. Try to feel the importance of the center here.

If it's difficult for you to keep your balance when you are lying on one side of your body, concentrate on lifting your weight out of your fingers and out of your toes. Don't let your weight fall down on the hip on which you are balancing.

Roll over on your back and relax for a couple of minutes before you turn over on your left hip and repeat the entire sequence.

Lifting Your Torso

The next movement demands abdominal strength, and repeating it is a good way to build it up. The goal is to perform the movements without any tension in your body other than the energy coming from your center.

Because the sequence works from a lying to a sitting position, then back, it's important not to divide it in two, but instead to use the image of climbing up a hill (rising up) and down (traveling down toward the floor) and then up another hill.

If you have had any back problems at all, or feel the slightest twinge of pain when trying this sequence, skip it and go on to the next.

Lie in a parallel position with your legs and feet extended. Begin the movement by imagining that a light ball is pressing your center down toward the floor. Then begin to raise yourself up into space by lifting *your head*, then *your shoulders*, then *your chest*, and finally *your waist* and *pelvic area*, until your torso is hanging over your legs. As you travel upward, imagine that you are traveling toward someone you know. Then, instead of staying here, curl back down again, maintaining the curvature of your torso. First sink *your pelvis* and then *your waist*, *your chest*, *shoulders*, and finally *your head*. As you travel down, imagine that you are slowly moving away from someone.

The main thing is to make the movement flow so that you don't get stuck at any one point but gradually slide from one point to the next.

Repeat the sequence 4 times, and finish with your torso over your legs. Try to relax in this position by "hanging" over your legs as you did in the Sitting Hamstring Stretch (page 53).

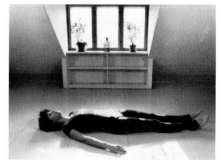

Lying-Down Combinations: A Wrap-Up

You are now finished with the lying-down part of the warm-up. You have been introduced to expressions such as *parallel*, *turned-out*, *extending* and *flexing* of the leg, *pointing* and *flexing* of the foot.

Try to bring with you to the following sections the most important experiences of this section: the connection between the various parts of your body and the way they influence each other; the awareness of the shapes that you create with your movements; the ability to stretch by directing energy toward the right places so that no surplus tension is at work in the body; and a better understanding of ways to send your energy out into space instead of keeping it locked inside.

This is a lot of knowledge to pick up at once, and I suggest that you continue to work with these sequences until your body feels ready to continue with the warm-up program.

Also, go back to the afspaending movements if any of the new movements are particularly difficult.

Before I continue, I'd like to introduce three new elements of modern dance to you. I've waited until now because there's so much else to think about when you're beginning to work with your body in relation to space, and there are limits to how much you can learn at one time. But what I'm going to discuss now can also be used in the previous combinations when you practice them.

1. Breathing

If your energy has a voice, then it must be breathing. By listening to your breathing, you can work with it to connect the wind power of your body to the external movements you make.

Lie down on your back in a relaxed position and place your hands on your stomach. Breathe in and try to send the breath down through your length axis, which you became familiar with in the afspaending section. By doing so, your stomach should lift itself lightly. Exhale the air immediately through your length axis, so that your stomach sinks as the air is let out.

Turn over on your stomach and try again. In this position your stomach is easily pressed against the floor.

Try not to hold your breath for longer than normal. The goal is to give you a little time to concentrate exclusively on breathing and to listen to it. Don't try to force your breath down to the abdominal region, but see how far down it can go on its own. As your body relaxes and energy begins to flow more freely, your breathing will naturally become deeper and calmer.

Remember that you should inhale through your nose and exhale through a slightly open mouth. Throughout the following warm-up, I will suggest specific breathing instructions that I hope will make the movements more complete in execution.

2. Rhythm

We are surrounded by life's constant rhythms. Some are free, irregular rhythms (the ocean's waves breaking), others are more regular or metrical.

Take the sound of a clock ticking: this sound is a steady pulse, similar to our own pulse. If the clock starts slowly to break down, a metrical rhythm will occur if one tick sounds louder than the next.

Rhythm adds variety and expression. This repetitive, precise sound defines time.

In the following combinations I will add time (given as numbers below each picture).

Begin by clapping a rhythm while you count, for instance, 1-2-3-4-5-6.

Be sure to maintain an even tempo, and repeat the rhythm many times.

Now add dynamics to the rhythm by clapping harder on one or more of the rhythm's beats.

You can, for instance, clap **1**-2-**3**-4-5-6, clapping harder on the accented beats **1** and **3**.

In the following chapters, the pictures are accompanied by numbers that show the rhythm. Sometimes there are two or more beats for one picture.

When you have become familiar with the movement combinations and have gotten a grip on the rhythm studies, you can begin to play with the rhythm's tempo, by slowing down or speeding up.

It's important that you don't end up tensing your body while concentrating on the rhythm. Always be aware of your breathing functioning calmly, freely, and evenly, even when you are concentrating hard and working energetically with the movements.

Return now to the last of the lying-down combinations. Give yourself plenty of time to study the rhythm information.

You will find the right tempo for the rhythm shown in the pictures if you listen to your own breathing and try to connect your inhaling and exhaling with the beats. Each beat represents one breath.

Don't feel like you're a slave to the rhythms that accompany the pictures. If in the beginning you feel limited by the rhythm shown, then do the movement first, later repeating it with the rhythm added.

You can also repeat the earlier combinations and make your own rhythm while you do the movements.

3. Focus

Focusing out into space instead of looking down will give your body an extra lift, and your weight will quite naturally follow an upward curve. In the following combinations you should al-

ways think about where you are looking, because it is an important step in getting your entire body on the right track.

It is important to become aware of your focus while moving, because it has a great influence on the balance of your bodily energies. If you close your eyes and try to move through space, you'll immediately notice how we depend upon our eyes for mobility.

In the following sections, your body will be up in space. Beware that you don't drop your energy by looking down when it is not natural to do so. Look out in front of you instead, and notice how your weight lifts up and stays there.

Movement Combinations: Sitting

Soles of the Feet Together

The next position we'll work with is a variation on the famous oriental pose seen in ancient artwork and known in yoga as the "lotus." In this position the groin muscles will be really stretched out because you are working in a turned-out position.

Remember, however, that you shouldn't *force* your legs into the position. If it hurts, bring your feet farther away from your torso so that the ten-sion in the groin area is lessened. It may help to work first with the af-spaending movement called Sitting Flower (page 34).

Sit in a parallel position with your legs stretched out in front of you. Rotate the legs out in the hip sockets.

Let the lower part of your legs slide up toward your torso by bending your knees and at the same time bring your feet toward each other so that the soles of your feet end up touching. As you bring your legs up toward your torso, try to feel that it is energy from your center that is moving your legs.

Afterward, do the movements in reverse, slowly letting your legs slide down into the turned-out position and then into the parallel position.

Repeat the combination 4 times, concentrating also on keeping your upper trunk lifted. End with the soles of your feet together. Relax your legs and upper trunk.

1

2

3

4

5

Look at the rhythm notations.

Repeat the combination one more time.

Your Arms

Now let us analyze the function of the arms, and see how they can help you in balancing the body. Here you can go back to the arm movements shown on page 22 as well as the Dynamic Forward Arm Stretching (page 41) for help.

In modern dance, we use the arms as one of the primary means of expression of such emotions as anger, love, and fear.

In order to communicate with the arms, it is necessary to be able to control them.

One of the most difficult movements is to lift your arms without raising your shoulders.

Place yourself as you were before, with the soles of your feet together, and straighten your entire back as you bring your shoulders down.

Now let your shoulders continue to drop into your back as you slowly lift your arms up to shoulder height. While keeping your shoulders down, let your arms slide slowly down by your sides.

Repeat the movement 4 times, and then relax by letting your torso fall forward and hang over your legs.

In the next combination, the impulse to move comes from your elbows, which you first bend slowly upward, after which you let your forearms follow in a flowing movement.

Now reverse the movement by dropping your elbows down toward the

1

1

2

2

3

4

3

floor and letting your forearms follow in the same flowing movement.

Repeat this movement 4 times and then relax by letting your torso hang over your legs.

87

In the next movement, you bring your arms directly out to the sides as an extension of your torso, after which you do a rotation with your arms.

Lift your arms as in the previous movement. When they are at shoulder height, look straight ahead, wriggle your fingers, and check to see whether you can see your fingers move while you're still looking forward.

If this isn't the case, then your arms are too far back, which makes your entire body sway forward, throwing your weight off your center axis. Bring your arms forward a little until you can see your fingers.

While you are holding this position, rotate your arms and hands from your shoulder socket until the palms of your hands point down. Then turn so that the palms of your hands are facing forward and then finally up. Be careful not to raise your shoulders.

Rotate your arms and the palms of your hands down, forward, and up 4 times, then let your arms drop slowly down alongside your body and curve over the legs so that your entire body is relaxed.

1

2

3

The Anchor

By letting your head act like an anchor, it pulls your torso forward and stretches your spine out, creating a curve in the torso.

Avoid a sinking feeling in your body when your torso travels over your legs. Instead, you should feel a lift upward, over, and down, rather than a sharp drop. Imagine while doing the movement that the energy is flowing out from the top of your head. This will help you to create a lifting feeling, even though your torso actually travels downward in space. Think of a ball that is thrown out into space and drops gradually to the ground.

Sit with the soles of your feet together and lift the weight in your torso. Let your chin fall down toward the upper part of your chest while you hold the lifting feeling in your body, and thereafter let the movement continue as your *head*, *shoulders*, *chest*, *waist*, and finally *pelvis* slide down. On the way down to the floor, let your arms follow the movement by bringing them in front of your knees.

Continue the movement by pulsing gently with your torso. Imagine that your torso has a slight case of the hiccups which is causing the movement down toward the floor and away from it again.

Come up again by lifting *your pelvis*, then *your waist*, *chest*, *shoulders*, and finally *your head* back up to a sitting position. At this point look directly out into space, wait 4 beats as you lift your weight, and then do the combination from the beginning again.

Try to get the rhythm in the movement and repeat it 4 times. Afterward, relax by lying down on the floor. The next combination examines more

1

2

3

4

1

2

3

4 and 5

closely the connection between your arms and torso.

Place the soles of the feet together. With a quick, sharp movement bring your arms forward and up with the palms of your hands facing outward.

Letting your arms rotate from your shoulder sockets, bring the palms up so that they face the ceiling, and then bend your elbows.

Imagine that your elbows are pressing the *center back* into space, and slowly follow the curve with your entire torso while your elbows approach center. Now your torso is curved, and your weight is located behind your center axis.

Move up again quickly and sharply via an impulse that originates in the lower part of your back, which should push forward in a slight arch. At the same time, *your waist*, *chest*, *shoulders*, and finally *your head* are again brought back onto the center axis.

Don't impede the energy by confining the movement to the shoulder area. Move your arms all the way from your back and connect the movement with the energy coming from your center.

Repeat the combination 4 times.

Swinging

Doris Humphrey and Charles Weidman were two innovators in modern dance. In the course of their joint work, they created not only new and exciting ideas in choreography, but also a series of movements that concentrated on the terms "fall" and "recovery." What you feel when you perform this technique is a freedom in your body that comes from big, sweeping movements that dive down toward the ground and reach up again into space. In the following sequences we will

1

2

3

4

and

5

work with a release and control of weight through swinging movements.

There are three elements in a natural swing: the *extension* of the body into space, the *release* of this extension in the body, and the repeated extension into space.

The point in these swings where you have to lose a little control is in the release. When you lose control, don't try to keep your weight down. Instead, use the swing's force to bring you up to a new extension.

Imagine the pendulum of a clock, which swings down and then immediately swings up again.

This movement is a continuation of the previous one, except that we add the swing, and your back is straight when you bring your torso forward from your hips. Use what you worked with in the Half-Sitting Pendulum (page 35) in the first section.

Sit with the soles of your feet together and lift your arms up over your head. Then bring your torso forward with a long, straight back. When you can't go any farther, let your torso curve and your head fall down toward your chest.

Return immediately to the beginning of the movement by performing the combination in the reverse order. Push from your pelvic region (arch forward slightly) and follow up and back onto the center axis with your torso in a straight line.

Repeat the combination 4 times, shake your legs out, and relax your body by lying down and really stretching out.

In this movement, the tempo is increased quite naturally because of the swings. Instead of the flowing movement we worked with earlier, you are

1

2

3

4

and

5 and 6

now going to try to find a more powerful movement each time you are down in the swing, and at the same time feel the sharp impulse behind the movement. Try the rhythm.

If you have problems with these movements, return to the previous combination where each movement was simpler and described in detail.

Sideways Stretch

I have already mentioned the image of energy flowing from the top of your head. In the next combination, try to maintain this image. Don't let the energy fall down, but instead let it shoot from your head and out into space while your torso performs a sideways bend.

Sit with the soles of your feet together, your weight directly on your center axis, and your arms out to your side.

Then lift your left arm up and out into space. Bring your left arm over your head toward your right side while you lean your head to the right. Your right palm is touching the floor, but don't press down on it. Use it to carry a little bit of your weight, just enough to hold your balance.

Be careful not to let your weight fall behind or in front of you.

Does your hand point directly into space in the same direction as your torso is leaning?

Continue the reach until you feel a good stretch running all the way down the left side of your back. Don't let your weight fall back into your right hip, but keep the energy alive by feeling that the side curve in your torso is extended.

Can you keep both buttocks on the floor and feel a stretch in your pelvic region? Keep the pelvic area focused

1

2

3

4

straight out in front of you; don't let it swing to the side.

The movement to return to the center position originates in the same place we started from. The muscles in the lower left side of your back pull your arm up over your center line, and the movement ends with your weight placed on the center axis in the center position.

Repeat the combination by lifting your right arm over your head, and reaching toward your left side.

Try the movement 4 times on each side.

Swing from Side to Side

The previous movements can be used to set your torso swinging. Now you'll combine a forward movement with the side movement by letting your torso fall to your side and slide forward and over to the opposite side, enabling you to draw a semicircle in front of you in space.

With the soles of your feet together, repeat the first part of the previous combination, bringing your left arm over your head and reaching out toward your right side.

Keep the stretch as you bend your torso at the waist and let yourself swing over your right knee. Continue to move toward the left side, passing through the center line at the middle of your body, and lift up on your left side.

Bring your right arm up over your head and back to your body's right side. The movement should start from the back, not from the arm itself.

Repeat the combination on the other side by letting your right arm reach over your head toward the left side of your body.

1

2

3

and

4

5

6

Try the movement at a slow tempo 3 or 4 times, and then add a powerful swing when you drop forward, passing through the center line. The tempo will naturally increase the moment the swing takes place.

Before you continue with the next combination, you should give your body time to relax.

The previous combinations with the soles of your feet together gave a good stretch to your groin muscles. You may become a little sore in this area for a while. That's because you're using parts of your body that you may not have used for a long time.

If you continue doing the movements on a regular basis, the soreness will disappear, and a feeling of openness and relaxation will take its place.

Forward with Stretched Legs

Now we will work with your legs stretched out straight from your torso. Try to feel your groin muscles when you are sitting in this position. If necessary, go back to the afspaending movement called Sitting Hamstring Stretch (page 53).

Bring your arms up in front of your body with the palms of your hands turned in, and move them forward in

space as you perform 16 light bounces. You will feel a stretch begin in your lower back. Because the movement starts in your center, you should reach out not only with your arms and head, but with your entire body.

Keep your back straight and feel how the energy is moving out through your feet and flowing out through your head.

Now flex your feet and make a forward curve with your torso. Imagine a gentle pressure on your center that doesn't press your weight down but encourages it up over your legs. Perform 16 light bounces, reaching out into space, and then slowly return to your starting position by placing each verte-

94

bra back onto the center axis, beginning with the lowest.

Shake out your legs and repeat the combination 4 times.

Also try the movements with your legs in a turned-out position. Remember that the rotation of your legs starts from your hip sockets.

1–16

1–16

Second Position

In the next position you will create a triangle in space by bringing your legs forward and out so that they face the corners of the room. This position is called "second position."

As the second position stretches both your legs and back, it may hurt a little in the beginning to sit like this. Don't force yourself; open your legs as wide as you can and no more. The stretches will eventually become greater and greater.

Keep your legs stretched in front of you in a turned-out position and keep your back straight. Now begin slowly to let your legs *slide* out away from each other as they approach second position. During this sliding, concentrate on your *inner* thigh muscles. Place your hands on them and feel how your muscles lengthen while you bring your legs out into space. Don't push with your hands.

Slowly return to your starting position by doing the movement in the opposite direction.

Don't strain your legs just to stretch them as far apart as possible. The goal is not to achieve a wide angle but to feel the stretch inside your thighs. Try to keep your back straight while you move your legs. That way you will also be able to feel the stretch in the lower part of your back.

Repeat the movement 4 times and finish off in an open second position.

Shake out your legs and relax your body.

1 2 3 4

5

Variations in Second Position

The numerous variations of second position all work toward making your thigh muscles more flexible, building up strength in the lower part of your back, and loosening up your groin muscles. In all the variations, your legs turn by the rotation in your hip sockets and your weight feels lifted, even if your torso is curved.

Give yourself plenty of time with these combinations. Feel where you are stretched, and where the energy is focused and how it flows in your body, as well as the precise points for tension and release.

First Variation in Second Position

Begin in second position, keeping your arms out to your side (this lengthens your back), and bend your right leg at the knee so that your right foot is flat on the floor. Slide your right foot in toward your center axis. When the sole of your right foot touches your left thigh, relax your foot and let it rest on the floor.

Hold this position and imagine that your pelvis is a face looking straight ahead into space.

Now reverse the movement as you open up out into space with your right leg. When you arrive back in second position, shake your legs out and do the combination by working the left leg.

Repeat the combination 4 times on each side, shake your legs out, and relax your body.

If your muscles are tight in this position, it may help to work with the afspaending movements Half-Flower, Lying Flower, and Sitting Flower (pages 34 and 46).

1

2 and 3

4

Second Variation in Second Position

In this variation you will direct your energy diagonally, using the corners of the room as guides.

Start with the sole of your right foot resting against your left inside thigh. Then, slowly twist from the waist over toward your left leg. Stretch your arms straight forward from your torso so that they are parallel to your left leg, with the palms of your hands turned in toward each other. With a fully lifted back do 16 light bounces straight forward in space so that the energy is sent out through your toes and fingers and your lower back is stretched.

Try to feel that you are reaching out after something in space. Imagine that there's something you'd like to have, and direct your eyes toward the diagonal. Make sure that your back and head don't drop while doing the bounces, which should ideally give you a feeling of lifting.

After 16 bounces with a straight back, repeat 16 times with a curved back.

Can you maintain a lifted feeling when your torso is curved?

Return to second position (see the first variation) and shake your legs out. Repeat the combination with the sole of your left foot against your right inner thigh, then repeat again 4 times on each side. End by shaking your legs out and relaxing.

Third Variation in Second Position

Now that you've worked with the two forward diagonals, try the two diagonals that go backward in space.

This time, create a straight line in space by reaching back with your right

1–16

1–16

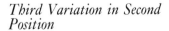

1–16

arm while your left arm reaches forward. This way you'll be able to feel the line of energy working forward and backward, traveling between your two arms in a line that runs across your chest.

Sit with the sole of the right foot against your left inner thigh and twist at the waist, bringing your arms parallel to your left leg.

Bend the right elbow and follow the movement through by bringing the right arm back across the chest and out behind you (see photo). Let your torso follow the movement so that you now face diagonally to the right. Keep this position for a moment while you feel the energy travel from one arm to the other.

Then perform 16 slow bounces forward toward the left diagonal. Return to second position.

Shake your legs out and repeat the combination on the other side, with the sole of the left foot resting against your right leg's inner thigh.

Repeat the combination 4 times on each side, shake your legs out, and relax.

1

2

3

1–16

Fourth Variation in Second Position

This variation repeats the stretch in your side and the feeling of energy flowing from the top of your head.

Again, the sole of your right foot is against your left leg's inner thigh. Begin with your left arm reaching out over your left leg and your right arm reaching backward.

Bring your right arm up over your head and twist from the waist toward the right diagonal. Bounce lightly 16 times with the lower side of your torso over your left leg.

Don't let your energy drop; instead, reach out into space.

Bring your right arm up and back, and twist back onto your center axis as you bring your right leg forward into second position.

Shake out your legs and repeat the combination on the other side with the sole of your left foot against your right inner thigh.

1–16

Variations on the Variations

You can do all these variations with a flexed foot so that the muscles along the back of your legs are also stretched.

The movement is done exactly the same way, except that you flex the foot of the working leg.

The three last variations can also be done with your leg bent behind you. This gives a good stretch to the upper thigh muscles of the bent leg. (Avoid this variation if you have had knee problems or feel any pain in the knee.)

Stretch in Second Position

You shouldn't do these stretches without having done the previous movements.

Sit in a narrow second position and lift the lowest part of your back.

Bring your right arm up and over your head and reach to the left side.

The energy should flow freely. Twist from the waist toward the right diagonal. Let your head follow the movement so that it is parallel to your left arm and leg.

Bounce gently 16 times over your leg and then return to your center axis.

Repeat the combination toward your right with the movement led by your left arm.

Shake your legs and repeat the combination with both feet flexed.

Stand Up

In the next combination you'll bring your body out into space where your weight and balance may be a little more difficult to control. As you move upward, feel your body grow up through space.

The combination is composed of many parts requiring concentration, and should be done in a flowing manner.

1–16

Sit with your legs extended and then bring your knees up toward your body with your feet flat on the floor.

Place your hands on the floor behind you and push forward with your hands, arching your back and flexing your feet.

Your back is now arched. Be careful if you have had any back problems. Let your weight come forward so that it is distributed between your hands and knees, and let your neck and head drop back gently. Try to relax in this position. It gives a good stretch to your thigh muscles and spine.

Push your weight away from your hands and let it move your torso forward as you catch your weight with the palms of your hands placed in front of your knees. Your torso forms a curve with your head toward the floor. Move your feet from a flexed position into an extended position by bringing the ankles back. Relax in this position before continuing.

Work yourself forward and up into space by flexing your feet, with the palms of your hands placed in front of you. Push off with your hands and feet. Let the impulse to move originate in your center and move your hands in toward your feet while you let your heels drop to the floor. Stretch the back of the knees. Both your feet and the palms of your hands are now on the floor; they all bear your weight evenly.

Let all your weight come back to your feet as you let go with your hands and bend your knees. Maintain the curve in your torso to protect your back and work yourself up, vertebra by vertebra, by lifting your *waist*, *chest*, *shoulders*, and finally your *head* back onto your center axis.

1

2 and 3

4 and 5

6

7

8

9 and 10

1

2 and 3

4

5 and 6

Come all the way up to a standing position. Standing on your center axis, finish off the combination while you count: 7 and 8.

Shake your legs out and relax your entire body.

Sitting Movement Combinations: A Wrap-Up

In this chapter we have begun to concentrate on coordination, which involves moving the body through space from side to side, forward, backward, and from one diagonal to the other. We have also begun to feel a faster dynamic through the swing, and to understand rhythm and the concept of moving from the center.

If you practice these combinations, you will be able to do the next section more easily. In the next part, your ability to remain balanced will depend on the strength you have acquired and your awareness of the importance of your center.

Before you start on the standing movement combinations, repeat the two previous sections until you feel you understand the movements thoroughly.

Don't get confused if your body doesn't understand something that your head understands. Familiarizing yourself with new ways to move takes far more time than understanding intellectually what you want your body to do.

WARM-UP 3

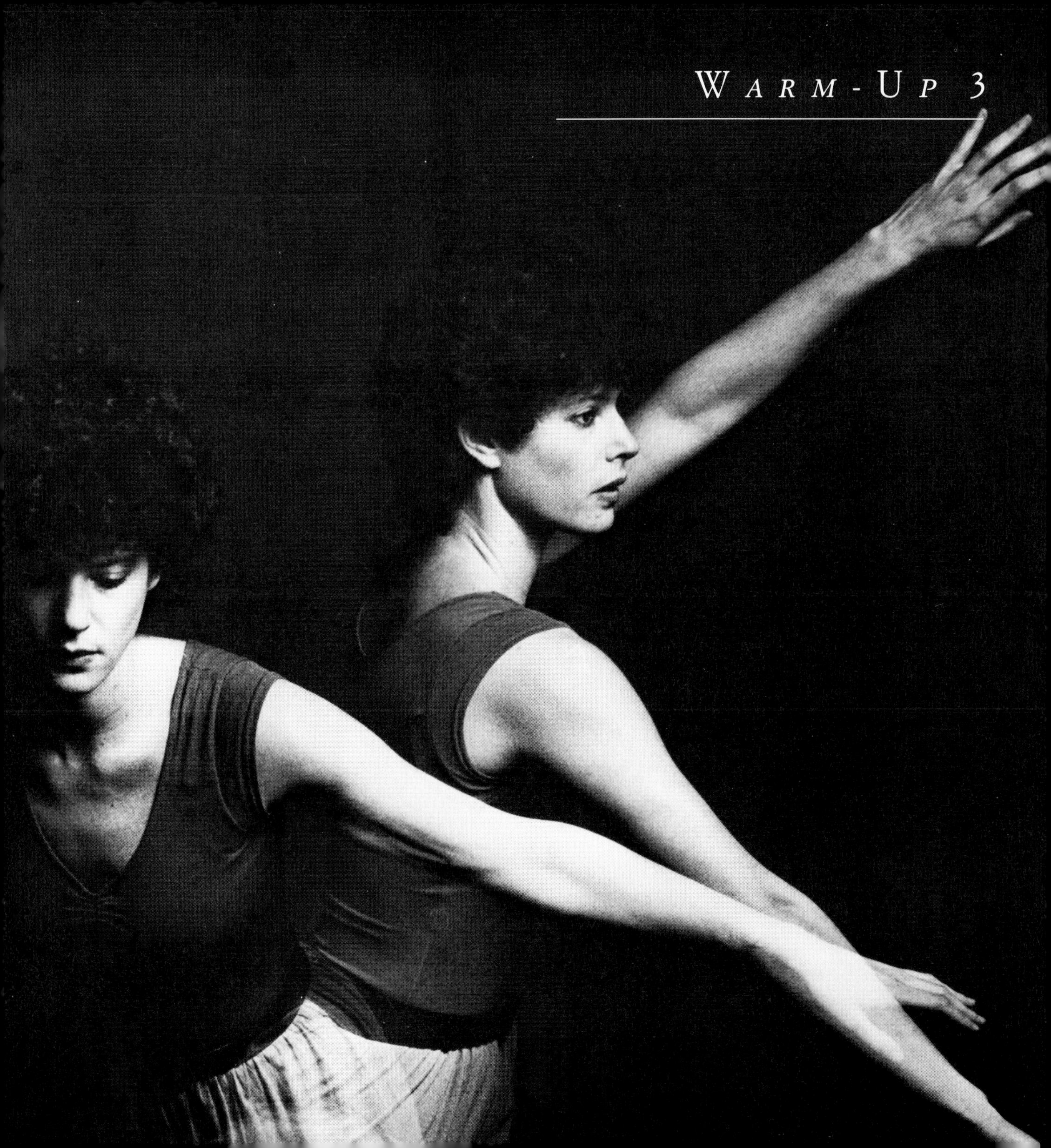

Movement Combinations: Standing

The following positions are the foundation for the standing warm-up.

It is important that you study the positions shown while you move from one to the other. You'll recognize many of them from the previous combinations.

First Position Parallel

Stand with your feet and legs together so that your hips, waist, back, and head are resting directly over each other.

If necessary, go back to the "Basic Standing Position" in the first section.

First Position Turn-Out

Keep your heels together on the floor while you rotate your legs from your hip sockets. Turn out as far as you can without altering your upper trunk. Let your body rest on your center axis with your weight equally distributed over both feet.

Second Position Parallel

Keeping your toes on the floor, turn out your heels by rotating your legs from your hip sockets until your feet and legs are lined up with your toes.

As you work your legs out and away from your torso, let your arms follow the movement.

Second Position Turn-Out

Keeping your heels on the floor, turn out by rotating your legs in the hip sockets until your toes point out at the same angle as they do in first position.

Again, let your arms follow the movement out and away from your torso.

Combine the Positions

Start in first position parallel, and move to first position turn-out with your toes, keeping your heels on the floor. Then lift your heels, place your weight on your toes, and slide out to second position parallel.

Repeat the movement with your toes and heels on the floor to second position turn-out.

Then reverse the movement from second position turn-out to second position parallel to first position turn-out to first position parallel.

Allow your arms to fall inward toward your torso.

Shake your legs out and repeat the combination 4 times.

Plié

Plié is French for "bend." In the standing warm-up we will work with the *demi-plié*, or half-bend, as we concentrate on *keeping our body's weight lifted in the torso, even if the body is moving downward in space.*

Two things happen in the course of a demi-plié. The ankles and knees flex and there is a slight flexion in the groin as the body sinks slightly and the entire spine is stretched.

1

2 and 3

4

1

2 and 3

4

Begin in first position parallel and slowly bend your knees, keeping your feet flat on the floor. This will give your body a firm foundation and help

you keep your balance throughout the movement.

Don't roll in or out on your feet, but rather keep your weight centered on

each foot.

Focus your attention on letting your bottom move straight down so that it functions as an anchor for your spine,

1

2 and 3

4

1

2 and 3

4

and keep your back straight—don't let it arch or curve.

Then slowly come up again to your starting position. Repeat the movement 4 times in all, and then repeat it 4 times in first position turn-out, second position parallel, and finally second position turn-out. Try to keep a slow, steady rhythm going through all four sets of pliés.

Shake your legs out and relax before you continue.

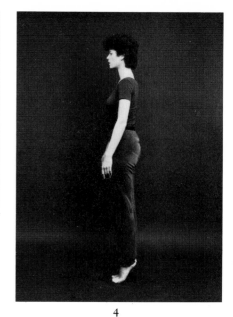

| 1 | 2 and 3 | 4 |

Relevé

Again, we will examine opposing movements, experiencing them through your body by performing them immediately one after the other.

We will now do the opposite action of the plié: the *relevé*, or "lift."

Begin in first position parallel. Keep your arms alongside your body and roll up through your feet until you are standing on your flexed toes.

As you move up to a complete relevé, your weight moves from the full foot to the half-foot and finally to the ball of each foot.

When you balance on your toes, make sure that your weight doesn't swing in front of or behind your center line, but rests directly on your center axis.

If there is to be any tension at all, it should be in your center. Don't let your weight drop; keep it lifted. Look straight ahead rather than down.

Count to 8 in this position and then slowly bring your heels to the floor.

When you come down on your full foot, don't let your weight drop down into your legs, but keep it rising in your torso while you imagine that your weight is lifting itself up out of your head.

Shake your legs and repeat the combination in first position turn-out, second position parallel, and second position turn-out.

Combine the Movements

The next combination is easy to understand if you have understood and felt the principles in the plié and the relevé.

Imagine that your body is a balloon that retains its lightness even when it's floating down to the ground.

Begin in first position parallel. Bend your knees to a demi-plié, then lift up through the starting position into a relevé. Return to the starting position.

Shake out your legs and repeat the combination in first position turn-out, second position parallel, and finally second position turn-out.

Remember that your weight should be placed on your center axis.

| 1 and 2 | 3 | 4 and 5 |

Your Leg Through Space

In the following combinations you'll work on keeping your balance by letting your weight shift onto the standing leg while your other leg works.

You'll need to keep your weight lifted up, or it will be difficult to keep your balance.

If you have problems with your balance, return to the first section and work on shifting your weight and balance (page 56).

Begin in first position parallel. Let your right foot slide out over the floor until your leg and foot are fully extended. At the same time shift your weight over to your left leg.

Bring your right leg back to the starting position and then behind you, with your weight still on your left leg. Let your body tilt forward a little.

Use your leg as if it were a cane that

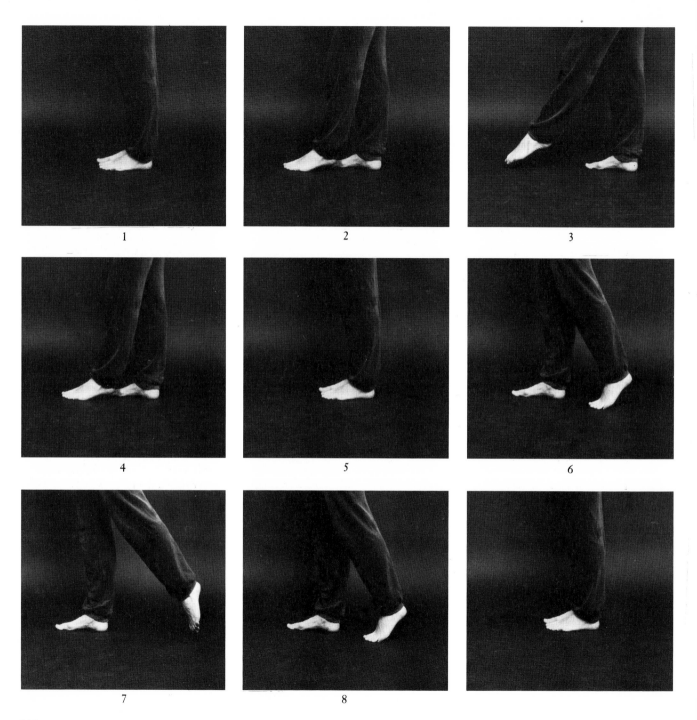

1   2   3

4   5   6

7   8

reaches and extends out into space.

Come back to your starting position, do a plié, and shake your legs out before you do the same movement with your left leg.

Repeat the combination 4 times with each leg.

Also try it in first position turn-out. Remember that the rotation of your legs takes place in the hip sockets.

Repeat the combination as you let the moving leg come off the floor a little. Make sure your torso doesn't lean as you lift your leg forward, but it should lean a bit forward when you lift your leg backward.

Leg Swing

You are familiar with "the knee reflex" from visits to the doctor. With a little rubber hammer, your doctor lightly hits your knee and your leg shoots upward.

The next movement resembles this reflex.

Stand in first position parallel and lightly hit your right leg in the crease separating the leg from the torso. Let your leg swing forward and up and then back to center position. Keep your knee flexed and relaxed while lifting the leg.

Avoid tensing your body as you lift the leg, and try instead to focus your attention on the energy that moves through your spine and forward along the back of your thigh to your lower leg and finally through your toes out into space.

Keep your torso on your center axis and be sure to keep your weight lifted out from your head.

Try this several times slowly, each time putting more power into the swing.

1

2

and

3

4

5

Now bring your arms up as you swing the leg, with the palms of your hands turned forward.

Repeat the combination 4 times with each leg, do a plié, and then shake out your legs.

When you feel that you can keep your balance and are familiar with the swing, try the movement with your legs in back of you. The basic principles are the same, except that you will move your torso forward slightly while swinging the leg back.

Repeat the combination in first position turn-out.

Swing with Stretched Legs

Lift your leg forward and up in a straight line. Think of your leg as an

1

2

3

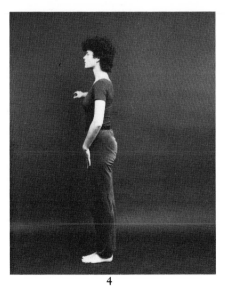

4

5

6

energetic line that moves lightly and freely through space.

Imagine that a strong wind is blowing from behind, lifting your leg forward and up. When you lift your leg behind you, imagine the wind blowing in the opposite direction.

Keep the standing leg stretched as much as possible. That way you stretch your entire body.

When you lift your leg, don't kick it up in the air—this will only bring your body out of axis. Instead, direct the leg in a sliding movement using the appro-

priate leg muscles.

Perform this movement slowly and carefully.

Repeat the positions in first position turn-out.

Swing Forward and Backward with Your Legs

Stand in first position parallel. Lift your left leg forward in one sliding movement, down again through your center line, and then backward and forward again, passing again through your center line. Don't divide the movement into a forward and backward movement, but connect the two parts like a pendulum movement. Notice that your torso comes forward a bit when your leg goes back.

Let your body work as a whole, and be sure to keep your hips, waist, chest, shoulders, and head aligned on top of one another, even though your torso is moving through space.

The first few times you do this combination you can use your hand to lift your leg. After a short while you won't need your hand to help, and you can lift your arm up and out at shoulder height.

Repeat the combination 4 times with your right leg, shake out both legs, and repeat it with your left leg.

Repeat the combination in first position turn-out. Remember to turn out your legs from the hip sockets.

1 and 2 and 3   and 4

5   6   7

Your Head as a Weight

The following movements warm up your back muscles.

Begin in second position parallel. Let your head fall forward as you bend at your knees, and follow it down with a flowing movement through your shoulders, chest, waist, and finally hips.

Reverse the movement, stretching your legs while returning to the starting position.

Do you feel your weight rising up in your body as you return to the center position?

Repeat the combination 4 times with slow, relaxed energy.

Standing Swing

What's exciting about doing these movements is that there comes a point where your body has to let go and relinquish control, or the movement will become stiff and the incomplete swing will be tense.

If necessary, go back to the Carousel (page 39) and the Ski Movement (page 43) in the first section. In the following combination, you'll see right away that the swing has to be big and free.

Once again, hold onto the feeling of your body being lifted, even though it's moving down toward the floor. Imagine you are floating in space, and use this image to give your body a feeling of weightlessness.

Start from first position parallel with your weight evenly distributed over both feet. Before you start, be sure that your hips, waist, shoulders, and head are in alignment.

Bring your arms up over your head as you stretch in the small of your back. Avoid lifting your shoulders up.

Now let your arms drop down with force and energy so that you curve your back and bend at your knees and ankles. Let the swing go all the way through and back, and let your arms swing all the way down to the floor and on up and behind you.

Keep the energy in the movement and let your arms drop down again and on up and forward, at the same time that you stretch your legs.

The two outer points in the movement are forward and up, and backward and up.

Repeat the combination 4 times, then return your entire body to your center axis and bring your arms down slowly

1

2

3

4

5 and 6

1

to your sides.

Shake out your legs and repeat the combination in first position turn-out as you bring your arms out to your sides and let them swing, crossing them in

front of your body at the swing's lowest point.

Repeat the movement in second position parallel and second position turn-out.

Remember that your arms form a cross in front of your body when you reach the lowest point of the swing in a turned-out position.

See the pictures on the next page.

117

1

2

3

4

5 and 6

ahead in order to concentate.

Repeat the combination 4 times and then bring your heels down to the floor.

Swing with Relevé

When you feel confident with the swings, go up to a relevé position. Lift yourself up on the balls of your feet with your body on its center axis, so you lean neither forward nor backward.

Drop down as the heels of your feet hit the floor; the knees and ankles flex as the torso curves. Swing back and up, forward and down, and forward and up as you come back to the relevé position.

In order to regain your balance, you must find your center. Focus straight

1   2   3

4   5   6

From Side to Side

Look again at the Side-to-Side Swing on pages 93–94. The next combination builds on the same principles, but now your weight shifts from one leg to the other through a second position plié.

Start turned out in second position and slowly stretch your body toward the right as you place your weight over your right leg and bring your left arm up over your head.

Stretch as far as you can, then swing down. When you hit the center line,

distribute your weight evenly over both legs before moving over to your left leg. Then bring your left arm over in front of your body and by using your back muscles, lift the torso up and back to starting position.

Use your concentration to help

gather energy again after the swing.

At first, this movement should be done slowly and carefully. After a while, as you feel increasingly familiar with it, you can set a faster tempo and feel the power in the swing when you fall through second position and pass your center line.

Reverse the movement by stretching your torso toward the left leg and bringing your right arm up over your head.

Shake out your legs and repeat the combination 4 times on each side.

Extension and Release

You are now going to examine the dynamics of extension and release by working with movements you make up on your own.

Any movement can be used. Just make sure you stretch out to an outer point, keep the position for a moment, release, and then move out again to another extension.

Give yourself images while you extend, release, and extend again. For example: You're a bird flying freely with your whole body extended. You see food down below, dive quickly, grab the food, and fly up again fully extended. Go on to create different movements using different images.

Torso and Leg Swings

This combination is long and complicated, and must be learned section by section.

Deecide for yourself how much you can take in at a time, and repeat the

1

2

various parts of the combination until you feel that you are ready to continue.

I suggest that you first read through the entire description in order to see where the tension in your body should be, how you should hold your arms, where your weight should be placed, etc.

Stand in first position parallel, quickly swing your right leg up, and then swing it down again as you quickly drop with the weight of your torso resting on both legs. Form a curve with your back and let your head function as an anchor.

Push up with the palms of your hands and come up and back to your center axis with your right leg up and out from your torso. Swing your leg

back, keeping your toes on the floor, and arch your back, your arms behind you. Swing your arms forward in front of your torso and lift them up as you cross them. Then come back to the center position as you keep your arms lifted high.

The combination begins from this point. Bring your arms down at the same time as you bring your leg up and repeat the entire sequence of movements.

Repeat the sequence twice, shake out your legs, and try the combination with your left leg.

Let your concentration follow the movement. When, for instance, the leg comes up, look straight out into space, not down. This will help your balance.

120

3

4

5

and

6

1

Standing Movement Combinations: A Wrap-Up

In this section you've concentrated on keeping your balance while lifting your leg, shifting your weight, working with more than one part of your body at a time, and controlling your movements without tensing your entire body.

Before you continue with the fourth and final section of the warm-up, be sure that you've understood everything you've learned so far.

Start your daily warm-up by lying on the floor and working upward through space.

It's particularly important that your body be warmed-up before you work with the movements in the next section.

Before and during each combination, ask yourself a number of questions:

Where is my weight when the movement begins, and when and where does my weight shift in the course of the combination?

Where is the tension point in my body? Does it move during the course of the combination?

If my arms are included in the movements, are my shoulders down?

What role does the center play in executing the combination?

What role does my center axis play in executing the combination?

Does the energy flow freely through my body, or is it locked in certain places? If it is locked, which movements from the previous combinations or from the afspaending movements can help release this excess tension?

When I move in space, is it clear to me how I move in relation to the surrounding space (forward, back, diagonally in front, diagonally behind)?

And the most important question of all: Does my body understand the movements, both mentally and physically?

Movement Combinations: Rhythmic

In this last section you'll move your entire body through space. I have described the movement combinations only very briefly because I believe you will be able to work with the movements by looking at the pictures and following the rhythms shown. Remember that your breathing should be free, deep, and steady.

First Combination

Plié as you drop your torso in front of your legs. Come up with your weight on your left foot.

Come back to first position parallel, and then bring your left leg forward as you let yourself drop down over it with your upper body. Catch your weight with your hands on the floor. Bring your right leg forward. Bring your knees up a little and stretch your back.

Come up to a standing position.

3 and 4 and 5

6 and 7

1 and 2

8

1

2 and 3

4 and 5 and 6

Second Combination

Drop your torso. Swing up with your weight on your right leg. Stretch backward.

Third Combination

Lift your right leg. Drop in second position. Come up and stretch out toward the diagonal.

1 and 2

3

4 and 5

1

2 and 3 and 4

5

Fourth Combination

Bend your head down and lift your
arms. Drop your torso. Come up with
your weight placed on your center axis.

| 1 and 2 | 3 and 4 and 5 | 6 |

Fifth Combination

Stretch your arms and torso to the left and your right foot to the right as you plié with your left knee.

Move your weight over to your right leg. Drop your torso forward on both legs.

Come up with your weight on your center axis.

Sixth Combination

Start in first position parallel. With a small, quick shift of your weight, move your torso over to your right leg. Then shift over to your left foot as you lift your right foot. These become tiny hops as the tempo increases.

1 and 2 and 3

Plié with your left leg and
stretch your right leg forward
so that you lean back. Shift the weight
quickly over to your left foot again, and
let your torso fall forward. Come up
with your weight on your center axis.

4 and 5 and 6 and 7

Bring your left leg forward and let your torso drop over.

8 and 9 and 10

Bring your right leg forward to meet
the left, and come up with your weight
on your center axis.

11 and 12

A Few Final Words

We could go farther with the warm-up combinations—turns, jumps, etc.—but because I'm not with you and can't guide you through the more complicated combinations, I'll stop here.

You can work for a long time with the combinations I have described here, and you will continue to experience new things as you become more familiar with them.

Every little movement contains so much to learn.

Further Reading

Modern Dance

Doris Humphrey. *The Art of Making Dance*. Evergreen, 1959.

Paul Magriel, ed. *Isadora Duncan*. Henry Holt and Company, 1941.

Don McDonagh. *The Rise and Fall and Rise of Modern Dance*. Dutton, 1970.

Yvonne Rainer. *Yvonne Rainer Work 1961–73*. The Presses of the Nova Scotia College of Art and Design and New York University, 1974.

Ted Shawn. *Every Little Movement*. Dance Horizons, Inc., 1954.

RHEA LEMAN was born in 1954 and grew up in New York City. She has taught modern dance since the age of 16 and has a B.A. in dance from the Boston Conservatory of Music. In 1976 she went to Denmark to work with dance and theater groups. She then spent some time at the Jacques le Coq School for movement and theater in Paris, and in 1981 returned to Denmark, where she started to work with Margit Haxthausen and to incorporate the concepts and practice of afspaending into her dance work. Today she is the leader of the dance group Teater Tango (formerly the Ladies) and works as a dancer and choreographer.

MARGIT HAXTHAUSEN was born in 1949 in Copenhagen and studied afspaending at the School for Holistic Afspaending, from which she graduated in 1975. She has had her own practice as an afspaending therapist and has also taught and treated mentally disturbed children. At present she is the head of the School for Body Therapy and Afspaending in Copenhagen.